Pass The Torch

Professional Development Workbook & Guide

"Pass the Torch of Knowledge"

2nd Edition

Sterling Mark, M.B.A.

Copyright © 2019 Sterling Mark- All Rights Reserved
All rights reserved. No part of this book may be used or reproduced by any means, electronic, photocopying, or by any information storage retrieval system without written permission of the publisher.

ISBN:
ISBN: 9781797511429

DEDICATION

This book is dedicated to the late Dr. Clement Glenn & Mr. Daryll Williams. These two men were both extraordinary servant leaders in their homes, communities and schools. They were extreme advocates for mentoring and building misguided young African-American males, like myself, to become community leader's and above all, MEN. Dr. Glenn & Mr. Williams also served Prairie View A&M University unconditionally, until they were laid to rest. I am very grateful that I had the opportunity to cross their paths in my life journey at Prairie View A&M University. They both played major roles in my personal and professional transition, at Prairie View A&M University.

Contents

DEDICATION i

ACKNOWLEDGMENTS v

Lesson 1 DEVELOPING A MINDSET TO CREATE GENERATIONAL WEALTH 1

Lesson 2 AVOIDING RISKY BEHAVIORS- THE UNFORESEEN 13

Lesson 3 MANAGING SITUATIONAL CONFLICT 22

Lesson 4 PERSONAL BRANDING 39

Lesson 5 RESUME & COVER LETTER BUILDING 48

Lesson 6 ELEVATOR SPEECH 57

Lesson 7 FIRST IMPRESSIONS 63

Lesson 8 DRESSING FOR SUCCESS 67

Lesson 9 "BEAST MODE" THE JOB FAIR 75

Lesson 10 MASTERING THE INTERVIEW 80

Lesson 11 INTRO TO FINANCIAL LITERACY 89

BONUS MATERIAL The Power of Mentorship 101

BONUS MATERIAL The Entrepreneur in You 107

ACADEMIC GRIND 119

RESOURCE PAGE 121

GLOSSARY 126

ABOUT THE AUTHOR 132

ACKNOWLEDGMENTS

In the first edition of Pass the Torch, I acknowledged my mentors and influential people that made a significant impact on my professional transition! Special thanks to: Vernon Mark Sr., Freddie Gibson II, Dr. Michael McFrazier, Dr. Terrance Finley, Dr. Lucian Yates III, Brother Frederick V. Roberts, Dr. Clement Glenn and Lee Gillian. These great men helped me transition into the professional entrepreneur that I am today. This second edition, I'd like to highlight EVERYONE that had a positive influence in my adolescence years! It took a village of people to raise me, and I highly appreciate everyone's efforts! I would love to list everyone individually, but I know you know who you are! Thank YOU!

Lesson 1
DEVELOPING A MINDSET TO CREATE GENERATIONAL WEALTH

"Every wealthy family had that one member that broke the chains of poverty for future generations."

~ Nicky Verd

In order to develop a mindset to create generational wealth, you must operate with purpose and passion while having a vision for the next phases of your life! You must have a sense of your family history and legacy while thinking optimistically towards adding to or creating your family legacy. If you don't know your purpose and what drives your passion, you will find yourself wasting a lot of valuable time that you'll never get back. Also, without a vision for the next phase of your life, you won't have a strategic outline for what you should be doing now to make that vision a reality. I remember my years of high school, being in class just to be a class clown- not focused at all! Many of us were in class because we had to be, not because we wanted to be. Back then, 2002-2006, I didn't have any passion nor drive and was living without purpose. I was stagnant with a ghetto mentality, and my focus was to survive day-to-day, and whatever else happened didn't matter. I had no outlook on the future or what it may hold for me. I was so fortunate and blessed to get accepted into college upon graduation, but since I still had no outlook on my future, all those negative traits carried over to my collegiate transition.

During my first three years of college, I was just another lost soul, building debt with no plans or thoughts of what my next move would be. I got caught up running with the wrong crowds and found myself being popular for reasons that were un-studious, which ultimately set me back as a scholar. "Why though?" You may ask. Truthfully, I never thought about nor asked myself, "Why am I in college" or "What am I going to do after college." If I would've asked myself these questions and answered them both in my freshman year, things would've started to click for me earlier in my transition to become a student. My transition to becoming a real student came in the year 2011. Five years had passed, and I had nothing to show for it. The other students that started college with me had either dropped out, graduated, or were in the same position as me, behind! I had cheated my way through so many courses, that when I got to the upper-level courses, I did not know how to complete the task or take the test. The test in the upper-level courses required not only the correct answer but a brief summary of why you chose that answer. I was completely mind blown and realized that it was time to buckle down and learn this information, or I was going to fail. Not only that, my family started to continuously ask me, "When are you graduating" and "Are you going to graduate?" I am so glad they did because they ignited my passion for graduating, and they ultimately made me realize my purpose for being in college. From that point, I began to seek out individuals and organizations that could help me be a better student and aligned with my personal goals. I found both when I met Brother Fredrick V. Roberts and Dr. Clement Glenn. They inspired me to join an organization named Collegiate 100, a subdivision to 100 Black Men. The young men that were part of that organization dressed for success strived for collegiate excellence and were known for making a positive impact in the local community. I quickly realized the power of mentoring in general, but peer mentoring seemed even more powerful.

I joined Collegiate 100 in 2011, and I graduated shortly after. Within that time frame, I found my passion through my family and found my purpose, which at that time was to graduate. During my time with Collegiate 100, I was educated on key techniques to stand out in the classroom like emailing the teacher before the course starts, dressing for success, sitting at the front of the class, answering questions and being prepared for class every day. I also learned how to network with professionals and the importance of beginning with the end in mind. One of the main takeaways I need you to understand with this part of the book is, the **power of receiving mentoring**! The older gentlemen that lead the organization held me accountable, disciplined me and taught me how to have principles for myself. Then the younger brother's in the organization provided daily peer mentoring in one way or another. I **STRONGLY** advise you to seek out two professional mentors and two peer mentors. Mentor's that motivate you to be better every day and truly care about your future and your success. Now, I know you may be asking yourself, "how do I pick or choose a mentor?" This is an excellent question, which can have many determining factors. I will provide some additional information regarding choosing a mentor later in the book (so look forward to it).

I was very grateful that I gained mentors, grew my network and learned those lessons from those gentlemen because after I graduated, I was faced with another hardship. I graduated with a bachelor's degree in Business Marketing, but I had no job. I felt the unemployment rate hands on, and the employers that were calling me in for interviews would be considered as underemployment. I moved back to Houston and found myself waking up every morning at 6:00 a.m. to check a site named Craigslist, to go and work for someone that needed help moving.

I followed this daily routine for almost two months, then one day I reflected on what I was doing to make money, and that's when reality hit me again. I realized that I was living and operating with no passion nor purpose again. I thought about how my family had fueled my passion for graduating from undergrad, and at that instance, it was clear to me. I needed to apply for graduate school, use my family and the people that cared for me as my passion, and my purpose would be for me to take full advantage of the opportunity and graduate with a master's degree and a career. I applied, and I was blessed to pass the GMAT test and get accepted into Prairie View's MBA program. This time around I knew how to utilize all the skills that I acquired after my transition to be a standout student and excel in the classroom.

During my pursuit of my master's degree, I found another passion and purpose. The summer of 2014, I was fortunate to land an internship as the first ever intern for the Office of the President at Prairie View University. I worked directly under the Vice President for Administration, Dr. Michael McFrazier. I was given a task to facilitate a program for incoming freshman men named Men Achieving Leadership Excellence (M.A.L.E.). I wasn't given any guidelines, so I was able to create this program to be unique. I worked with Mr. David Hughes, we developed the theme for the program, and from there I insured every aspect of the program would be dynamic and realistic. While facilitating this program, I found a passion for speaking to students and empowering them with the knowledge I had obtained from my failures & successes. The purpose was clearly to assure that they didn't travel down the same path that I took and to let them learn from my mistakes so that they could be successful without wasting years of their life and building debt.

When the program ended, I received so much feedback from the students about how much they liked it and how it changed their lives. This gave me a feeling of satisfaction like no other! With the program complete, I had to continue with my initial end-goal in mind, and that was to graduate with my M.B.A., and with a career. So I stayed the course and found an opportunity to take part in the Thurgood Marshall Leadership Conference, which is where life as I knew it changed for me. One of the most important key notes that I learned during my transition was, with every task or opportunity I needed to define my passion and purpose for that specific opportunity beforehand. This ultimately kept me level headed and gave me a tunnel vision to complete whatever the situation may be, which you should do as well. When I learned about the atmosphere that the Thurgood Marshall Leadership Conference would have, I told my roommate the night before I left "I am about to go up here and change my life!" There is no way you can put me in an atmosphere where employers are looking for unique students like myself, and I do not know how to deliver results. I went to the conference with a passion to be sharp and impressive, and the purpose was to leave with a career that could change my life.

I left the Leadership Conference with three job offers. I was very gracious that at this point and time, I only had one class left to take in my degree and it was online, so I could relocate if needed. I had a job offer from Kellogg's to be a territory sales representative, and the option to move to either: Ithaca, New York, Savannah, Georgia, or Lakeland, Florida. I also had an entry-level position offer with the FBI that would be located in Houston, Texas. Lastly, I had a job offer with Walmart Logistics to be an Area Manager located in Smyrna, Delaware. I took the offer with Walmart due to a great offer, and I would start in a managerial role, which would be a greater leadership experience.

I worked for Walmart for almost two years, received two promotions, and it was truly a great experience. Then one day, I wound up finding myself thinking about my passion for educating the youth, and the purpose was greater than any achievement I had attained. February 2016, I acted upon my passion and walked into my purpose. I started my own business, Sterling Empowerment, and began to reach out to schools, groups, and organizations that serviced economically disadvantaged minority youth, in need of relatable empowering workshops. Starting my own business really opened my eyes to a bigger picture in life, which was **ownership**! In order to create generational wealth, you must **own** assets and have **residual streams of income**! This mindset was mainly important because I began to think about passing generational wealth to my family, which added another level of purpose to my life.

The key learning from this chapter are if I never would've found my passion, I never would've found a purpose of graduating. I never would've found the purpose to go back to college and pursue an M.B.A., which I graduated with a 3.4-grade point average. I also never would have had the opportunity to find a new passion and new purpose, that's bigger than anything that I could imagine, which is to empower and pass the torch of knowledge to all.

Below I have four exercises for you to complete. Please fill them out honestly so that you can prepare for your own future right now and start the process of developing a mindset to create generational wealth.

The first exercise, I want you to briefly write out two (or more) major mistakes that you or someone you know made, that changed **your** life (for the worse). Next, write out the impact that it had on you.

Mistake Made	Impact Felt

Thanks! In the next five blanks, I want you to briefly write out the most important lesson(s) you learned from the mistakes, and how it changed your view on life (for the better).

Great! That exercise was to make you aware of the mistakes that you cannot make again and to take in what you learned from those mistakes. Be aware that we all make mistakes; we just have to use them as learning eras in our lives and not take any steps backward to repeat those mistakes.

The next exercise, I want you to think about and write down what it is that you want to do with your life and what do you want to be. Close your eyes, think about what is it that you could do in this world, that you could do every day and do this for free. Although, I don't want you to think I want you providing services for free, what I want you to understand is that anything you can see yourself doing every day for free, you must have a unique gift to do it and it could ultimately be or lead you to your purpose in life. Many people measure success by the amount of money someone has or a job title, but what they don't realize is that some people get paid six-figure jobs because they have **found a solution to a problem.**

Can you think of a problem that you know many people deal with that you have a passion for fixing? Be realistic! So close your eyes, think, visualize it, and then write it down.

The last exercise, I want you to think about and write down all the people **YOU would let down if you didn't succeed**. Think about the people that you know care about you the most. It can be family, friends, mentors or anyone that have helped you get to the point where you are today.

Thanks! The people whose names that you just wrote down are the people that are going to drive your passion for fulfilling your purpose. No matter what task, project or job it is, you can always refer to the thought of doing it for those people and it will drive you to take your energy to the next level. Also, you must remember to approach each task with the understanding of what's going to drive your passion and the purpose of the task, to guarantee you stay aligned with your goals. The moral of that story is, **ALWAYS KEEP YOUR PASSION FRESH!**

Lastly, let's think about creating generational wealth. What does the thought of owning and creating a business that generates wealth look like to you? What family members (or close friends) do you love so much, that you always want to make sure they're taken care of when you're not there?

In the next few blanks, write down why you think it's important to create generational wealth for your family. Next, write down who you think could benefit from you becoming successful and creating generational wealth.

Why is it important to create generational wealth to you?

Who you think could benefit from you becoming successful and creating generational wealth?

Now that you've found something that you're passionate about and have a deeper understanding of how you can impact your family generationally, your goals could lead to your life purpose! Speaking for self, I use the pain that I feel from having a broken family and never meeting my father, I use as daily motivation to fuel my passion to fulfill my purpose. No matter what, you must remain RESILIENT! You have many options in this day and age to create generational wealth, with the assistance of the internet and technology. What's very key for you right now, is making sure that you eliminate the risk that's involved in your life. No one wants to be dead or in jail because of a situation that could've been prevented by proactively thinking. The next chapter will cover risky behaviors. You've already past the first level of empowerment so let's carry on; you're doing great!

Lesson 1 Review Notes

Lesson 2
AVOIDING RISKY BEHAVIORS- THE UNFORESEEN

"Life is inherently risky. There is only one big risk you should avoid at all costs, and that is the risk of doing nothing."

~ Denis Waitley

While searching for quotes to fulfill the mission of this chapter, I came across that one and loved it. I loved it because it has so much truth that I immediately related with, because there is risk in doing nothing. Some people don't realize that opportunities pop up for everybody all the time; that's the way we progress. It's whether you're in the right frame of mind or the right stage of your life, which determines whether you see them. Taking unnecessary risks are never the safest option, yet the safe option sometimes can be the worst option. For example, allowing yourself to be influenced to do what everybody else is doing because it's trending, or not moving away for college because you can stay close to home. In this section we're going to cover the behaviors that may be unforeseen harm or risk to your future, which you must avoid to stay on track.

We're not going to discuss the most obvious behaviors like carrying drugs-weapons or fighting. You should know there's a negative consequence that comes with those behaviors every time! We're going to discuss the unforeseen risks that can sometimes be overlooked, starting with influence.

Ask yourself, "WHO" and "WHAT" are you allowing to influence you? This is a critical piece to your future success, because like "they" say, birds of a feather flock together. Which means, more than likely whatever your friends are into, you may be as well. Allow me to make this simple. If your family member/boyfriend/girlfriend/friend(s): are abusive, play video games all the time, watch TV all the time, want to sleep all the time, only care about looking like a BOSS/DIVA, only care about being seen in Instagram & Snapchat, are self-centered, sell or do drugs, like being involved in mess & drama, or has no vision for their future, YOU DON'T NEED TO HANG WITH THEM! I don't care if it's your sister, cousin or brother, you cannot afford to be side-tracked by someone who is not on track, PERIOD! People that consistently look to engage in those types of behaviors, and are in love with the street life, could have you depressed or in jail, simply because you were there with them. You must remember if you're hanging with someone that doesn't care about their freedom, what makes you think they're going to care about yours?

This chapter is crucial because if you're not conscious of these risky situations & behaviors, you could be inheriting a risky behavioral mindset, which will develop into bad habits. I grew up around all of it which is why I'm so determined to help you avoid these traps. At one point and time in my life, I remember my alarm clock being my mom dropping ice cubes in a glass at 6 am to start drinking liquor. I also remember my mom always going to a friend's house to drink and smoke all night (on school nights). This place had homeless people and junkies there all the time, doing some sort of drugs and drinking alcohol until they passed out or violence broke out. If a child lives and grows up in an environment where drugs, alcohol, drama, and violence are the norm, it's a high possibility that the child will believe that he/she will naturally become a product of that environment. This was the case for me. Fourth grade was the year that I believed cigarettes were just a part of life, so I started stealing cigarettes from my mom and smoking them when she left. No one made me aware of the harmful side of these events, as a kid, if you see more liquor stores in your community than libraries, it becomes even more natural to see yourself engaging in these activities.

Another risky behavior that I allowed myself to be influenced by is the party-life. I watched my mom and older cousins go out to the party, and it led me to want to do so as well. The party-life behavior is something that I need you to keep a hold on, and I will explain why. Students that go to college and have never been exposed to partying/drugs/weapons, and are easily peer pressured, are highly likely to get involved negatively in some form or fashion. I can remember going to parties where the people who were throwing the party gave out free "pre-made" drinks. What they didn't tell people was that they were crushing up pills and putting them in the drinks. People would start drinking and not know why or how they wound up passed out. I also knew three people personally that died in college, from being at a party or hanging out after the party was over. You must understand that the majority of people that are partying are possibly under some kind of influence of drugs. When people are under the influence and out in front of what they may consider a lot of people, they tend to feel like they have something to prove. Then all it takes is something as simple as stepping on somebody Jordan's, and somebody ends up getting shot, or a fight breaks out. Not to mention, now all the people who are drinking and under the influence are now driving their cars back to their destination. Now you have to be extra careful on the road because the drive home will be even more dangerous. I'm not telling you this to scare you or stop you from going to parties, all I am saying is be selective of which parties you want to attend. School parties held by departments are a pretty safe bet. Parties that are family oriented or parties that are given by parents of friends are safer as well. Majority of issues with parties happen at the off-campus parties, where there may not be any type of security or protection for all in attendance.

Now let me ask you a question. Do you think you can be influenced by music? Do you think that consistently listening to music that talks about drugs, violence, sex, and drama all the time can be a risky behavior? I do believe so! I believe so based on my personal experiences with the music that I listened to during different phases of my life, compared with the lifestyle I was living during those times. Certain music I listened to promoted discriminating women, the use and distribution of drugs and violence. Although I do understand that some artist paint pictures of their reality, I didn't realize that it made me feel more comfortable to engage in those activities, as well engage with other people who have accepted the lifestyle of self-destruction. My prime example of this is with myself. I'm from Texas, and in Texas, we have our own culture of music. The music artist that I idolized promoted: driving Cadillac's on swangers (these are rims that has an 84' inch diagram), getting a gold/diamond grill put in your mouth and surviving the streets. I started listening to this type of music in the 3rd grade, so by the time I was in high school I was stuck and in love with that lifestyle, which transpired to bad habits. I was so influenced that I truly believed living that lifestyle was an example of success, this mentality carried over into my college years. It wasn't until I was exposed to scholars and professionals that I realized, there are other ways to live life peacefully and successfully. Living the lifestyle of a "ghetto star" eventually led to me almost losing my life. I had a guy try to rob me at gun point for my car, which was a Cadillac on swangers. At this time, I was supposed to be a student, preparing myself for the next phase of my life. Unfortunately, **I was still caught up in trying to look good for people that didn't care about my life nor had a vision for their future.**

The last item I want to cover regarding music and its influence, is sex education. This is very important because there are many songs that promote sex recklessly, yet they don't tell the whole truth which can be misleading to the youth that listens. Many songs promote unprotected sex but don't discuss the fact that by having unprotected sex you put yourself at risk to contract diseases such as HIV, herpes, syphilis, chlamydia, HPV, etc. If only one side of the conversation is being promoted in songs, the youth that listen and don't have an outlet to have conversations about sex, will be misled about sex education. I try to inform youth that people that engage in this risky behavior should not be your role model. Having unprotected sex also leads to unplanned/unexpected pregnancies, and if you look at the statistics, youth are contracting diseases and having children at extremely younger ages. If the youth are having babies as teens, more than likely they are financially unstable to take care of themselves and the child. Not only that, many of those relationships do not transpire to marriage which means more kids are growing up in single-parent homes and poverty. This is what regenerates and continues the cycle of generational poverty.

What about sexting? What is sexting you ask? Sending or getting sexually explicit photos, videos, or messages through your cellphone or online. Sexting is risky because it can have legal consequences like child pornography charges or having to register as a sex offender. Online photos also live forever and can get into the wrong hands, which can be used to hurt you and be shared without your consent. In order to prevent this behavior, take these precautions: protect yourself and others by not taking sexually explicit pictures or videos, speak up when someone makes you uncomfortable with their texts or what they send you and respect others by not pressuring them to sext you. If you receive a sext: delete the picture or video, share your concerns with someone you trust, or report a sext that was sent to you or shared without your consent to the Cyber Tip Line.

Below I'd like you to write down the most important learnings from this chapter:

Next, write down all the risky behaviors that you know you engage in, that could be a potential harm to your future and life:

Lastly, write down the actions you can take to eliminate the unnecessary risk:

Thanks! This is one of the first orders of business that you must get in line for you to maximize your potential and live a long successful life. Next, we will cover managing situational conflict.

Lesson 2 Review Notes

Lesson 3
MANAGING SITUATIONAL CONFLICT

"Raise your thoughts, not your fists."

~ Matshona Dhliwayo

There are two approaches to managing situational conflict, proactive and reactive. Knowing how to manage conflict is very important and will be a major key to your success because conflict happens daily. Once you realize that your future success is more important than the conflict that's happening now, you'll find techniques to diffuse the conflict while achieving your desired outcome. Let's cover the proactive techniques first!

In order to be proactive to a conflict, you must raise your level of awareness of giving and receiving verbal and nonverbal communication (ex. body language). There are four basic styles of communication: Aggressive, Passive, Passive-Aggressive and Assertive.

Aggressive Communication is a style in which people express their feelings and opinions and advocate for their needs in a way that can violate the rights of others. Thus, aggressive communicators can be verbally and physically abusive. Aggressive communicators will often:

- Try to dominate others
- Use humiliation to control others
- Criticize, blame, or attack others

- Be very impulsive
- Have low frustration tolerance
- Speak in a loud, demanding, and overbearing voice
- Act threateningly and rudely
- Not listen well
- Interrupt frequently
- Use "you" statements
- Have an overbearing or intimidating posture

The impact of a pattern of aggressive communication is that these individuals:

- Become alienated from others
- Alienate others
- Generate fear and hatred in others
- Always blame others instead of owning their issues, and thus are unable to mature

The aggressive communicator will say, believe, or behave like:

- "I'm superior and right, and you're inferior and wrong."
"I'm loud, bossy and pushy."
- "I can dominate and intimidate you."
- "I can violate your rights."
- "I'll get my way no matter what."
- "You're not worth anything."
- "It's all your fault."
- "I react instantly."
- "I'm entitled."
- "You owe me."

- "I own you."

Passive Communication is a style in which individuals have a pattern of avoidance. They fail to express their opinions or feelings and fail to protect their rights. As a result, passive individuals do not respond overtly to hurtful or anger-inducing situations. Instead, they allow grievances and annoyances to mount, usually unaware of the buildup. But once they have reached their high tolerance threshold for unacceptable behavior, they are prone to explosive outbursts, which are usually out of proportion to the triggering incident. After the outburst, however, they may feel shame, guilt, and confusion, so they return to being passive. Passive communicators will often:

- Fail to assert for themselves
- Allow others to deliberately or inadvertently infringe on their rights
- Fail to express their feelings, needs, or opinions
- Tend to speak softly or apologetically
- Exhibit poor eye contact and slumped body posture

The impact of a pattern of passive communication is that these individuals:

- Often feel anxious because life seems out of their control
- Often feel depressed because they feel stuck and hopeless
- Often feel resentful (but are unaware of it) because their needs are not being met
- Often feel confused because they ignore their feelings
- Are unable to mature because real issues are never addressed

A passive communicator will say, believe, or behave like:

- "I'm unable to stand up for my rights."

- "I don't know what my rights are."
- "I get stepped on by everyone."
- "I'm weak and unable to take care of myself."
- "People never consider my feelings."

Passive Aggressive Communication is a style in which individuals appear passive on the surface but are acting out anger in a subtle, indirect, or behind-the-scenes way. People who develop a pattern of passive-aggressive communication usually feel powerless, stuck, and resentful – in other words, they feel incapable of dealing directly with the object of their resentments. Instead, they express their anger by subtly undermining the object (real or imagined) of their resentments. Passive-Aggressive communicators will often:

- Mutter to themselves rather than confront the person or issue
- Have difficulty acknowledging their anger
- Use facial expressions that don't match how they feel - i.e., smiling when angry
- Use sarcasm
- Deny there is a problem
- Appear cooperative while purposely doing things to annoy and disrupt
- Use subtle sabotage to get even

The impact of a pattern of passive-aggressive communication is that these individuals:
- Become alienated from those around them
- Remain stuck in a position of powerlessness
- Discharge resentment while real issues are never addressed so they can't mature

The passive-aggressive communicator will say, believe, or behave like:
- "I'm weak and resentful, so I sabotage, frustrate, and disrupt."
- "I'm powerless to deal with you head on so I must use guerilla warfare."
- "I will appear cooperative, but I'm not."

Assertive Communication is a style in which people clearly state their opinions and feelings, and firmly advocate for their rights and needs without violating the rights of others. These individuals value themselves, their time, and their emotional, spiritual, and physical needs. They are strong advocates for themselves while being very respectful of the rights of others. Assertive communicators will:

- State needs and wants- clearly, appropriately, and respectfully
- Express feelings clearly, appropriately, and respectfully
- Use "I" statements
- Communicate respect for others
- Listen well without interrupting
- Feel in control of self
- Have good eye contact
- Speak in a calm and clear tone of voice
- Have a relaxed body posture
- Feel connected to others
- Feel competent and in control
- Not allow others to abuse or manipulate them
- Stand up for their rights

The impact of a pattern of assertive communication is that these individuals:

- Feel connected to others

- Feel in control of their lives
- Are able to mature because they address issues and problems as they arise
- Create a respectful environment for others to grow and mature

The assertive communicator will say, believe, or behave in a way that says:

- "We are equally entitled to express ourselves respectfully to one another."
- "I am confident about who I am."
- "I realize I have choices in my life, and I consider my options."
- "I speak clearly, honestly, and to the point."
- "I can't control others, but I can control myself."
- "I place a high priority on having my rights respected."
- "I am responsible for getting my needs met in a respectful manner."
- "I respect the rights of others."
- "Nobody owes me anything unless they've agreed to give it to me."
- "I'm 100% responsible for my own happiness."

Being assertive allows us to take care of ourselves, and it's fundamental for good mental health and healthy relationships. Assertive is the top choice out of all the communication styles for me. It's direct, strait to the point and clear. Next let's cover conflict management and resolution techniques, which would be the reactive approach to managing situational conflict.

Conflict Management is the process of limiting the negative aspects of conflict while increasing the positive aspects of conflict. The aim of conflict management is to enhance learning and group outcomes, including effectiveness or performance in an organizational setting (Ra him, 2002, p.208).

Students, when you arrive at college, you will face several conflicts that you have never come across before. For most of you, the reason will be because you are now in a new environment that you have never been in or not accustomed to. For others, it will be because you will place yourself in environments that endorse conflict, which could ultimately make you a victim of "wrong place at the wrong time." Furthermore, with the understanding that we will always face conflict unforeseen at times, we have to know how to manage the conflict at hand effectively.

For students that are transitioning to college, the first thing that you need to comprehend and fully understand is that you are now officially **on your own**! No one is going to wake you up for class or make you go to class. You've already paid for the classes, so every class you miss is money that you're throwing away. Let me break it down for you a little more and give you a scenario. Let's say that you are registered for five courses in one semester, and your tuition for that semester is $15,000. Let's also say that you have to attend each class 25 times in that semester. $15,000(tuition)/5(number of courses) = $3,000 per course. Now take that $3,000(per course) and divide it by 25(number of classes), which equals $120 per class. So every time you miss a class, you're throwing away $120 that someone has spent their hard earned money on. This number, $120, is a very cheap example of how much money can be lost. This just another reason why you have to value each class and understand that you have already invested in yourself. You can't be out there playing all the time, thinking that college is all about having fun. To some, being on your own and fully responsible for yourself may be a conflict, but to others, this may be an opportunistic challenge. Speaking for myself, I was on my own after my sophomore year of high school, but I wasn't making the right decisions because I was unaware of the information that I needed to be successful. I was stuck in my ways, not thinking, which carried over into my collegiate transition. So for me, not being aware created a personal conflict that extended out for years.

Another important key that I need you to take notice of is that you need to be precise about who you allow in your circle of influence. This is very important! You should not constantly hang out with people that: make fun of you, do not go to class, do not have any goals, do not believe that you will be successful, and/or use drugs and alcohol. You must surround yourself with positive, champion minded people; People who motivate you to be a better you. Lastly, you should associate yourself with people that have more knowledge than you in other areas that you're not familiar with, so that you can be more knowledgeable. You know what they say, "Birds of a feather, flock together!" Which means you are who you hang around, and if you hang around smokers you're most likely to be one, so don't get caught up in the hype.

Below are a couple of common conflicts that will arise as you matriculate.

Common Conflicts:

Personality Differences
Personality differences can and will occur anywhere! Whether you're: in class, at work, at the store or a friendly game of kickball. For example, you may be the quiet, laid back type and like to be around people who are not loud mouths and likeminded. Whereas, someone else may like to talk a lot and be around people who always speak their mind. These two different personalities will bump heads.

Language Barriers
Language barriers can happen anywhere as well. In higher education, you will quickly realize that there are a lot of teachers from different origins that are professors. When I had this conflict, I found utilizing the teacher's office hours very handy! Teachers love to see a student passionate about understanding. This was still a conflict because if I can't understand the teacher, how can I understand the information to pass the class.

Also, employers recruit talent from different states and backgrounds, especially if the company promotes diversity. So now you would need to know how to work with diversity daily, which if you can't it'll become a conflict.

Age Differences

Age differences will happen in the classroom (College especially) and work. There will be older students who have either started school after pursuing their career and students that are returning to school after some time.

Working with people will also include age differences. I'll use myself for example. At 27, I was a manager over associates that were over 40. Then, of course, my superior operational managers were older than me, but only by a few years at 35. With that age variance, you have to be careful with how comfortable you get with people so that you're not viewed as a friend.

Different Opinions

Everywhere you go people are going to have different opinions, especially if it's always been a hot topic. For a prime example, "whose greater, Michael Jordan, Kobe Bryant, Magic Johnson or LeBron James?" This question alone will cause a conflict that could last for decades!

Another example may be, "Who would be a better president?" I am sure that this will bring out all types of opinions.

Roommates

Whether you're at home sharing a room with someone you know or in college sharing a room with a stranger, having a roommate imposes conflict that could be very harsh. This is one conflict that has to be managed assertively.

Next, we will take a look into the different types of conflict management styles, and the advantages and disadvantages of using them

Conflict Management Styles:

Accommodation (Smoothing): Smoothing is playing down the conflict and accommodating the concerns of other people first, basically putting your personal feelings to the side.

Below are a few examples of when an **accommodation** would be advantageous or appropriate to use, and a few disadvantages or caveats:

Advantages (Appropriate Use):
  i. When the issue is more important to the other person than it is to you
 ii. When you know that you are wrong
iii. When you know, the other person is argumentative, and the issue could get harmful

Disadvantages:
  i. The other person may try and take advantage of your tendency to accommodate; they may view you as an easy push-over
 ii. If you consistently use this tendency, you may seem afraid or unconfident when facing someone who is over aggressive
iii. People may not turn to you when it's time to make an executive decision, because they may feel that you won't stick behind it if confrontation arises

Collaboration (Problem Solving): Collaboration involves an attempt to work with another person, searching for a solution that meets each other's needs. This could ultimately be a win-win situation for both parties, resulting in a mutually beneficial result.

Below are a few examples of when **collaboration** would be advantageous or appropriate to use, and a few disadvantages or caveats:

Advantages (Appropriate Use):
　i.　When you care about the person, and you don't need to have any animosity as a result
　ii.　When you are looking to work out a long-term relationship with a person
　iii.　When you are working in groups and everyone's opinion matters

Disadvantages:
　i.　It may require more exertion and effort to come to a resolvable solution, depending on how many different peoples input is involved
　ii.　Time may be of the essence, and a quick solution or response may be necessary, which could be hard to come about depending on how many people are involved
　iii.　Everyone that is involved in the collaboration has to mutually accept the collaborative solution for it to work

Compromise: Compromising is bargaining for gains and losses to each party; this style of managing conflict looks for a mutually accepted solution that satisfies both groups.

Below are a few examples of when **compromising** would be advantageous or appropriate to use, and a few disadvantages or caveats:

Advantages (Appropriate Use):
　i.　If time is of essence, compromising may provide a faster solution
　ii.　Compromising may offer a temporary solution while looking for a more effective solution
　iii.　Compromising alleviates the stress and tension between both people temporarily

Disadvantages:
  i. May result in no solution if a mutual agreement is not met
  ii. You may be blind to some facts, and the other person will take advantage of your tendency to compromise
  iii. If you are dealing with a salesman or shark, you may need someone who is an expert negotiator or someone who has more knowledge of the situation, to converse and compromise for you

Avoidance (Withdrawal): Avoiding is denying the existence of the conflict and hiding your true feelings. It's completely acting as if the whole situation doesn't matter to you.

Below are a few examples of when **avoidance** would be advantageous or appropriate to use, and a few disadvantages or caveats:

Advantages (Appropriate Use):
  i. When you know that the issue isn't worth arguing or competing against
  ii. When you know that it's not the right time nor place to discuss the issue
  iii. When you know that you're not prepared enough to compete, which would give you more time to collect information

Disadvantages:
  i. This may make you look weak as if you're afraid of confrontation
  ii. If you are depended on to speak up or act, this may negatively affect your relationship with the people that are expecting you to take action
  iii. People may view your avoidance to a particular subject as rude and cold-hearted

Competition (Authoritative Command/Forcing): Competition is basically forcing your concerns or solutions, despite what the other person thinks or feels.

Below are a few examples of when **Competition** would be advantageous or appropriate to use, and a few disadvantages or caveats:

Advantages (Appropriate Use):
  i. When people are procrastinating, and a decision has to be made
  ii. When you need to defend yourself or stand up for a friend that's less authoritative
  iii. When you need to resolve a prolonged conflict with someone that you care about

Disadvantages:
  i. Could affect your relationship negatively depending on the person and subject
  ii. If the other person has an authoritative conflict management style, this could lead to further and harmful conflict
  iii. The person or people may perceive you to be a push-over

This sums up the common conflicts that may arise and the different conflict management styles. Next, I have three exercises for you to put the management styles into use.

The first exercise I'd like you to write out which conflict resolution skill you would use with the common conflicts and scenario given and why:

Personality conflict:
Language barrier conflict:

Age difference conflict:
Different opinions conflict:
Roommate conflict:

Next, I want you to write out two major conflicts that you've had in the past. Two conflicts that you know **YOU** could've managed better and had a better result:

Good job! Now that you've written out those two conflicts, first I want you to identify and write out the **initial** conflict management style you used, then identify the alternative conflict management style that you **should've** used to resolve the situation.

Initial Conflict Style:

Alternative Conflict Style:

Great job! It's very important to identify these types of situations. It's vital to know and understand what went wrong and what you could've been done differently, that would've made a positive impact. Study these different conflict management styles so that you can be mentally prepared for whatever conflict that arise.

The next chapter will cover Personal Branding.... Let's Go!

Lesson 3 Review Notes

Lesson 4
PERSONAL BRANDING

"Your brand is a gateway to your true work. You know you are here to do something – to create something or help others in some way. The question is, how can you set up your life and work so that you can do it? The answer lies within your brand. When you create a compelling brand, you attract people who want the promise of your brand – which you deliver."

~ Dave Buck

Personal branding is the process of creating a unique personal perception that others will perceive as your reputation. Personal branding can be based on your: characteristics, personality, passion, uniqueness, drive, abilities, strengths, and the results that you ultimately achieve.

The goal for personal branding should be to build your reputation with specific unique qualities so that when people seek for the service that you provide, they will actively pursue you due to the expertise and knowledge that you have in that particular field.

Let's review a few key processes that will assure you to build a phenomenal personal brand.

Firstly, you need to know and understand what your career goals and aspirations are. Think about what you want to do with your future. It's very important to have an idea of what you want to do with your future because if you don't, you could fall victim to anything or anyone. Get a visual of where you want to see yourself 5 and 10 years from now. There's plenty of people that are going to answer this question with a general answer like, "I want to be rich 10 years from now", but how? Nowadays there are students pursuing majors like Social Work and Visual Arts, which are two of the lower paying majors, but they are expecting a six-figure career because they have a degree. That's why it's very important to research majors and careers and to have at least an idea of what you are hoping to do in your career.

Now think about your aspirations, goals, and dreams. How can you attain these? If you want to attain your goals and dreams, you have to act on them! That's the only way! (This kind of goes back to finding your passion and pursuing your purpose which we covered in chapter one) I can't think of anyone who's achieved their aspirations by doing nothing, and if they did, it didn't mean anything to them because they didn't have to make a sacrifice or go on the hunt to get it!

Now that you know what your goals are and what you want to do with your life begin with the end in mind! For example: If I wanted to be a Motivational Speaker, I would go and find the gurus of motivational speaking and study them. I would learn their professional background and the steps they took to get where they are at now. I would seek ways to meet them and form a personal relationship with them, or someone close to them. The bottom line is that I can learn from the mistakes that others have made on the rode to their perfection, and implement my uniqueness, ultimately creating my brand.

Next, you need to see yourself through a different set of eyes. Think about how people perceive you. It's always best to get feedback from someone who can be bluntly honest. Take a look at the way you act, speak and dress through the eyes of those around you. Do you have your own unique style, or do you just follow the general population trends? Who are you seen hanging out with after class and on the weekends? You want to be aware of these situations because being seen with someone that has a bad reputation could give the wrong impression about you.

One of the key aspects of personal branding that some people overlook is the messages and pictures that they are posting on social media sites. This is very important because social media posts can make or break your career! Companies now have Social Media Specialist that will look you up on all social sites and know who you are and how you think before they meet you in person. You should always be mindful and very careful of what you say, and how you say anything that's being displayed to the general public! Speaking of public, when you go out in public or to class, be mindful of the image you give through the clothes that you wear. You may have to ask yourself, "Am I dressed like I want to go to class today" or "Do I look prepared for greatness today?" You may find yourself walking back to the closet if you realize that you are not. It's time to start living and dressing a little more professionally and strengthen your brand.

It's now time to find what makes you unique! One of the first things to do when building your brand is to understand what makes you unique. Ask yourself, "Why am I different from the other students in my major, as well as other people in general?"

Write your answer down in the text box below.

It's important to understand what makes you unique. Although employers are judging you by the decisions you make, they are also looking for candidates that are unique. You may find doing a personal SWOT Analysis of yourself helpful. SWOT Analysis are your: Strengths, Weaknesses, Opportunities, and Threats. It's an honest inventory of your characteristics, which can be used to your benefit.

You can fill out your SWOT analysis below:

Strengths:
Weaknesses:
Opportunities:

Threats:

Now that you know your strengths and weaknesses, you should build a strong skill set to increase your weaknesses and utilize your strengths to take advantage of the opportunities that come available.

These skills can be academic, professional, social or otherwise. Either way, the more skills you can become an expert on, the more credible you become. Credibility is very important in building your brand. The more credible you are, the more likely an employer or person will feel they can trust you and the skills that you can offer to a job. In the next chapter we will discuss soft vs. hard skills to get an in-depth look at different types of skills, but for now, let's finish up mastering our brand.

Ever heard the phrase "Build your network, and build your net worth?" It's very true! You always want to take advantage of any, and every opportunity you have to network and be identified. You may not realize it, but you are already networking with people! Anytime you talk to someone in class, join a new organization or sit next to someone on the bus; there is potential for networking.

It's very key to network with professionals, to get your name into the professional world as well. Network with your teachers, your parent's friends, and anyone else that you can because you never know who can connect you to your dream career! Remember, the more you network, the more connections you will have that know and can talk about you and can refer you if they feel that you are credible for the task.

Now that you have all this personal branding knowledge, it's time to get involved and market yourself! Get involved with campus activities and organizations, which is one of the easiest ways to meet people and opportunities. By getting involved, you allow yourself to have a foundation of clientele, and at the same time, a good set of people who will be willing to help you. Marketing yourself is not the same as sharpening a skill or meeting the right people; you must have multiple streams of awareness that you are here and why you are here. If you want to be known as the student with the barber business, do more than just cut hair! Take photos, develop business cards, and embrace a professional social media presence and get to work! This is really when all your social media skills can come to play and make you stand out from the rest in your field. Download multiple social media sites: Facebook, YouTube, Instagram, Tumblr, LinkedIn, Twitter & Snapchat. If you're thinking about starting a business, be sure to make two profiles to separate yourself from your business. It's great to keep up with your family and close friends on your personal page, while also having a designated page to market your business and build business brand awareness.

We've discussed a few pros for using social media for marketing, now let's cover some of the cons. Some people don't realize that they may be fired before they get hired for a job depending on their social media. For example, let's say I'm an employer and I'm looking to hire someone immediately for a photography position. I have two people that have submitted very impressive resumes, Jack & Jane. They both have similar experiences based on their resume's, which forces me to look for another outlet to get to know them better before I choose to pay them $60,000 a year. This is when I would turn to social media to see what kind of online brand they're presenting, to make sure that their online presence represents my company, since my company has an online presence as well. First, I take a look at Jack's profile first. He has a profile pic up with his friends, a few of them have their shirts off, and one of them has cigarettes and a beer. I look at his post, and he has curse words and negative messages that don't represent what my company stands for. Then, I go and look at Jane's profile. Her profile shows that she has been posting pictures of different graduation photos that she has completed with her friends. Jane also has posted pictures of her taking photos for her church and school organization. Based on the two profiles, which do you think I would pick to pay $60,000 a year to represent my company well? Jane of course! So make sure that you remember that a social media profile can be very beneficial to you and your brand, or it can cause someone to avoid you.

Now you are ready to shine! Remember, although this is YOUR brand, you wear the last name of your family. So, anyone that doesn't know your family or where you're from, your personal brand is a representation and reflection of those people! So make sure that you represent well! Also, keep in mind that there are a lot of students that are going to graduate from all over the world every semester that will be in the field that you desire. You must make sure that you are phenomenal in every aspect of your brand and ALWAYS find ways to stay a step ahead of your competition so that you can remain relevant and everlasting!

The next chapter we will cover resume building and take a look at a few different hard skills and soft skills that will help build your resume to stand out

Lesson 4 Review Notes

Lesson 5
RESUME & COVER LETTER BUILDING

"The internet was supposed to make this whole business of job searching rational and simple. You could post your resume and companies would search them, and they'd find you. It doesn't seem to work that way. There aren't enough jobs for experienced, college educated managers and professionals."

~ Barbara Ehrenreich

Developing Your Resume

Your résumé exists for one reason, which is to help you stand out from the crowd! Your chances to land a job will improve if your résumé meets the job criteria. Nowadays, you also want to keep in mind that depending on the career you're seeking, that job may require specific formatting for your resume. So definitely do your research, and below I will give you the standards that you can utilize and build on.

You want your resume too clearly:

- Explain your career objective
- Show chronologically the places where you have been employed
- Present a clear picture of the positions held
- Outline your accomplishments

- Detail your education and skill sets
- Show graduation date/degree (or anticipated date)

You want to develop a professional, crisp and clean resume. "How do I do that?" Make sure you have proper spacing and margins, make sure that all words are grammatically correct and make sure that it's a maximum of two pages.

Make sure that you also include a tailored career objective to the specific position that you are applying for. A career objective is a statement positioned at the top of your resume. Any statement of more than two sentences is too long. To be effective, the career objective must catch the reader's attention and suggest why you are applying for the job.

Here is a link that you can follow that will give you the perfect model to follow, and it's very easy to use: https://www.resume-now.com

Also, be mindful that if you're not comfortable with using Microsoft Word or need assistance with formatting, there may be a writing center on your campus that can assist you and if not, there are professional people online that can help you. I like to use Fiverr.com for a lot of my writing needs. They are good and very affordable!

Building a resume that stands out above the rest of your competition is very imperative. A resume is one of the first initiatives to impress recruiters, so it's key to understand how to build your hard and soft skills to become an expert with a specific niche. Next, we will cover hard skills vs. soft skills.

Hard Skills

Hard skills may include tangibles like a degree or certificate. Hard skills are also teachable skills like software programming or facilitating spreadsheets. These skills are more technical and will help you get the job you are seeking. Here are a few listed below:

- A degree or certificate
- Typing speed
- Machine operation
- Computer programming
- Proficiency in a foreign language

Soft Skills

Soft skills are skills that are personal attributes. These are skills that are personally gained through experiences and will ultimately help you keep the job, versus getting the job. Here are a few listed below:

- Teamwork
- Communication
- Patience
- Time management
- Motivation
- Presentation skills
- Facilitating
- Leadership
- Mentoring/Coaching
- Negotiation
- Networking

Soft skills are skills that can be worked on, acquired or come naturally. Speaking for myself, I have a natural motivation, but that's not something that I can go and get a degree in or be taught. Some people have it, and some people don't! Soft skills differentiate people that may be in the same job field or with the same degree. That's exactly why it's very important to have soft skills in collaboration with hard skills because they are a necessity to rise above the competition. It all goes back to knowing exactly what it is that you want to do, then you will know exactly what skill sets to build so that your resume will show that you have a niche for that position.

In the exercise below, I want you to write out five skills that you **know** you have. It doesn't matter whether they are hard or soft, just make sure that these are skills that you have obtained:

Thanks! Now I want you to think about the career that you want to pursue. Then, I want you to analyze the skills that you have just written down… Now think about the skills that you need to obtain to be the guru in your profession. This may require you to look the position up again if you didn't earlier, but this will help you have a tunnel vision for exactly what you need to do to flourish. So write down all the skills that you **need to obtain** and build on, to shape you and your resume for that dream career:

Great Job! Now don't just write this down and let it be just another thing in the past. It's time for you to develop and enhance your skills so that you can be the best that you can be! Let's continue to the next phase of building your resume to stand out.

Complete Internships

Completing relevant internships to your dream career will be very beneficial to you because you'll now have relevant experience. Also, when you are speaking to recruiters or an interviewer, you will be able to speak their lingo which would create an interpersonal relationship. You may even land a job at the place where you landed your internship. According to a scholarship.com article, "Even if your internship doesn't result in employment with that company, it still gives you the chance to see what that job is like and have an idea of how it's performed within a professional setting. You may even find your internships change your mind about your career goals, either focusing them or redirecting them towards something that works better for you." They are correct! You may have wanted to pursue a career in administrative education, then land an internship as a principle in training and realize that you would rather be a teacher.

Now that you know this information seek out relative internships online and at job fairs that will perfect your craft. Also, be mindful that you don't have to wait until your junior or senior year of college. The earlier, the better!

Work /Volunteer/Intern

For most students, college is the last time in their lives that they are no longer required to work. Choosing to take free time and give it to charities, organizations, and fraternities show compassion and commitment, two things that will be valued by a variety of employers. Volunteering is also a great way to get linked into a career while gaining relevant industry experience. The greatest thing about it, I believe, is that if you volunteer in high school or college at the job that your considering for a career, you actually get to: see what it will be like to work day to day in the real environment, and you may even realize that you like a different position that the one you thought primarily. With this experience, you won't be the student that falls victim to going to college for 4-6 years, then going into a career that you'll end up hating.

Also, for those that do acquire campus jobs or jobs that may not be directly related to your field, don't think that these jobs don't matter. Even if they are irrelevant in your career field, jobs in retail or on campus can illuminate your work ethic, longevity, and loyalty, and use that position as a reference.

Another way to build your resume is seeking out class projects that will look good on your resume and impress employers after graduation. I took a business marketing class that required us to do a service-learning project. This project required a business plan, which required primary research and other types of hands-on learning opportunities. We also got to shoot a marketing video, which was fun and creative. I was able to put this project on my resume to show employers that I had experience researching, developing surveys and creating financial budgets.

The last strong key to building a resume that I would like to discuss is submitting your resume online, which is knowing how to get through the filter.

For example: If I wanted to get a job with Accenture to be a consultant, and I knew they are hiring for that specific position. I would go to the job description and qualifications, look at some of the key vocabulary terms that they use, and find places in my resume that I have relevant experience to replace with their terminology. This can help you get your resume through the internet filter, and from there you have the power to get the interview.

Also, remember that a resume should be one page. If you have a lot of different job experiences, it will be best for you to create different resumes with the relevant experiences related to the job you are seeking. For example: If you are seeking sales positions, put all of your sales jobs on one resume. If you're seeking an educational administration position and you have a lot of job experience doing that, create another resume and put all those experiences there. There is nothing wrong with creating two or three styles of resumes because it's best to uniquely tailor your resume for the specific position that you are seeking.

The last item that I'd like to make you aware of that works together with your resume, will be a cover letter. A cover letter is a document sent with your resume to provide additional information on your skills and experience.

The letter provides detailed information on why you are qualified for the job you are applying for. Don't simply repeat what's on your resume, include specific information on why you're a strong match for the employer's job requirements. Think of your cover letter as a sales pitch that will market your credentials and help you get the interview. As such, you want to make sure your cover letter makes the best impression on the person who is reviewing it.

A cover letter typically accompanies each resume you send out. Employers use cover letters as a way to screen applicants for available jobs and to determine which candidates they would like to interview. If an employer requires a cover letter, it will be listed in the job posting. Even if the company doesn't ask for one, you may want to include one anyway. It will show that you have put some extra effort into your application. Effective cover letters explain the reasons for your interest in the specific organization and identify your most relevant skills or experiences. Determine relevance by carefully reading the job description, evaluating the skills required and matching them to your own skills. Think of instances where you applied those skills, and how you would be effective in the position available. It would be wise to use Google to view cover letter templates and examples before creating one.

Wow! You are making great progress! A few more chapters and you'll be ready to go out and be the most professional person that you can be!

The next chapter we are going to cover the elevator speech. This will be a short presentation that you will find very useful in many situations. Let's check it out.

Lesson 5 Review Notes

Lesson 6
ELEVATOR SPEECH

"The purpose of an elevator pitch is to describe a situation or solution so compelling that the person you're with wants to hear more even after the elevator ride is over."

~ Seth Godin

Have you ever found yourself walking alongside someone that you knew was important and could be a great professional networking connection, but you didn't know what to say? You didn't know the proper way to greet the person, or you feared that the person was on a tight schedule and may not have the time to have a fully engaged conversation. This is where your 60/90 second elevator speech comes in handy. It's very key to get this perfected because this type of interaction usually isn't planned and it's normally your first impression, so you must be sharp. The interaction with this certain person usually happens by fate, and normally that person is pressed for time which means you need to be precise, directly to the point, and make an everlasting impression.

Please take note of the knowledge I am giving you below.

This short verbal presentation should:

- Be a personal advertisement for you and your resume
- Highlight your skills, strengths, and education
- Demonstrate your enthusiasm, personal brand, and abilities

The presentation can market you effectively in a variety of situations such as:

- Random and planned networking
- Social occasions
- Job fair
- Interviewing

Below is an example of my 60/90 second elevator speech:

"My name is Sterling Mark, and I am a graduating senior, majoring in business with a concentration in Business Marketing at Sterling University. For the last four years, I have worked off campus at a small local retailer part-time as an intern, in charge of marketing to a group of vendors.

I have learned a lot about vendor marketing & I look forward to joining a progressive organization like yours where I can use my current skills to be successful as a Marketing Trainee.

Outside of school, I am an active volunteer with my church's outreach program, and I also work with my fraternity weekly to mentor students in the community. I am also active in the Marketing Club and have been chosen to mentor freshmen business students who aspire to have a career in Business Marketing.

I am seeking career opportunities outside of my current employer because they are unable to add additional employees at the time when I will receive my degree in May of this year.

I would like to be considered for opportunities within your organization strongly. Is it okay if I get a card or contact information to follow up with you?"

Now, I would like for you to write down your 60/90 second elevator speech. This may require you to review your resume to be precise.

Great Job! Now that you've written it out, it's time to practice it! Practice it with your friends, a teacher, or anyone who is willing to give you constructive criticism. Remember that practice makes perfect, so let's make sure that you are prepared at all times to impress.

Speaking of impressing, next we will cover First Impressions, then move to Dressing for Success. You've done great so far; lets continue this empowering journey!

Lesson 6 Review Notes

Lesson 7
FIRST IMPRESSIONS

"You never get a second chance to make a first impression."

~ Andrew Grant

The truth is, first impressions, can leave a lasting impression! When I was a freshman in college, I dressed like a hoodlum which gave the impression of a hoodlum. I am sure anyone who remember back then, remembers that I wore: clothes that were too big, a stocking cap on my head and gold teeth. That impression that I gave to people still affects my image this very day!

When I received the internship to be the intern for the Office of the President at Prairie View A&M University, after my studious transition, I had a lady see me that remembered me very well from back then. The first words she said when she saw me were, "Look at God!" I completely blew her mind when she saw me in a suit, nice dress shoes with a clean cut. It was then that I realized how important it was for me to be sure to have a great first impression on people because it could be your last chance to have an impression at all!

During my scholarly transition, I also learned how key it was to make an impression on my teachers and employers. The tips that I am going to give you will put you ahead of your competition, whether it's the classroom or pre-interview.

Tip #1: You only have one opportunity to make a first impression. Whether it's an interview, first day of class or random networking, you should always be prepared, dressed for success and ready to impress

Tip #2: With interviews and class, it's very important and the key to make a good first impression **BEFORE** you meet face-to-face

Tip #3: You can do this by sending an email or linked-in message expressing your gratitude. My personal experience with this, specifically with teachers has been phenomenal. By reaching out first and before class starts, the teacher now has the opportunity to have a personal relationship with you and will recognize you first, whenever class starts.

Now that you understand the importance of making an impressive first impression, it's time to make sure that you are dressed for success every time the opportunity presents itself!

Lesson 7 Review Notes

Lesson 8
DRESSING FOR SUCCESS

"Your appearance is your expression to others about who you are and what you stand for. The way you look reflects your self-image, attitude, confidence, and state of mind. A strong, purposeful presence is the hallmark of an effective image."

~ Natalie Jobity

Dressing for success in college can be vital to your brand, as well as the first impression you make in the classroom. Sometimes you have to get dressed, look in the mirror, and ask yourself, "Am I dressed like I want success today?" If you're going to class in pajamas, basketball shorts, flip-flops or curl rollers still in your head, the answer is more than likely NO!

Here we will cover the different styles of dress wear for men and women by the occasion.

White Tie

Women
- Formal (floor length) evening gown
- Long gloves (optional)

Men
- Black tailcoat, with matching trousers

- White piqué wing-collared shirt with stiff front
- Shirt studs and cufflinks
- White Vest
- White bow tie
- White or gray gloves
- Black patent shoes and black dress socks

Black Tie

Women

- Formal (floor length) evening gown
- Dressy cocktail dress
- Your dressiest black dress

Men

- Black tuxedo jacket and matching trousers
- Formal (piqué or pleated front) white shirt
- Shirt studs and cufflinks
- Black bow tie (silk, satin, or twill)
- Black cummerbund to match tie or a vest
- No gloves
- Black patent shoes and black dress socks

Semiformal

Women

- Short afternoon or cocktail dress
- A black dress
- Long dressy skirt and top
- Dressy separates

Men

- Dark, business suit
- Matching vest (optional)
- Dress shirt
- Tie
- Leather dress shoes and dark dress socks

Business Formal

Women

- Suit
- Business-style dress
- Dress in a jacket
- Stockings
- Heels, low or high

Men

- Dark business suit
- Matching vest (optional)
- Dress shirt
- Conservative tie
- Leather dress shoes and dark dress socks

Business Casual

Women

- Skirt, khakis, or pants
- Open-collar shirt, knit shirt or sweater (no spaghetti straps or décolleté)
- Dress

Men

- Seasonal sports coat or blazer with slacks or khakis
- Dress shirt, casual button-down shirt, open-collar or polo shirt
- Optional tie
- Loafers or loafer-style shoes, and socks

Dressy Casual

Women
- Dress
- Skirt and a dressy top
- Dressy pants outfit
- Nice jeans and a dressy top

Men
- A seasonal sports coat or blazer, and slacks
- Dress shirt, casual button-down shirt, open-collar or polo shirt
- Optional tie

Casual

Women
- Sundress
- Long or short skirt
- Khakis or nice jeans
- Shorts (depending on occasion and climate)
- Plain T-shirt (no slogans), polo shirt, turtleneck
- Casual button-down blouse

Men

- Khakis or good jeans (clean, no holes)

- Cargo or Bermuda shorts—depending on occasion and climate
- Plain T-shirt (no slogans), polo shirt, turtleneck
- A casual button-down shirt and sweater
- Loafers, sneakers (with or without socks), sandals

After researching this subject, I found that the Emily Post Institute at emilypost.com gave the best overall information, so I want to recommend you to their site. I'd also like to refer the fellas to take a look at http://www.realmenrealstyle.com/mens-dress-code-transcript/. They have style courses that will take your dress game to the next level! Big ups to Mr. Antonio Centeno and thanks for the resourceful information.

For the ladies, I was able to find a nice photo that will give you a visual of the proper dress for success attires. This photo can be found at http://macroccs.com/wp-content/uploads/2014/07/dress-codes-womens-page-001-1024x630.jpg.

Below are some standard fashion tips or the "starter kit" that can apply to men and women.

Standard Fashion Tips *(Men and Women)*

- Shirts: 2 oxford button down (white) 1 navy button-down; 1 white French cuff
- Trousers: 1 black; navy; brown; khaki
- 1 navy blazer (2 buttons)
- 1 black or navy suite (2 buttons)
- 1 pair of black and brown dress shoes
- 1 reversible black/brown belt

These were standard fashion tips given to me by the great Dr. James Wilson Jr. I met Dr. Wilson during the summer of 2014, and this is one man that can dress like no other! I was able to learn a few things from him that summer, so I want to show my appreciation by referencing him for this stylish knowledge.

Now, I know what you're probably thinking. These clothes will cost a lot of money. That just depends on where you're shopping. If you're on a tight budget like myself, allow me to make a few suggestions on where to shop. This is going to sound crazy, but Goodwill. Go to a Goodwill that's located in a nice (rich people) area. If you go to a Goodwill in an area where the rich people live, you'll be able to shop for the clothes that they have donated, which may be very nice stuff. Once I found out this secret, I found Polo blazers and nice slacks for $3-$10 apiece, in great condition. You can also shop at Thrift shops/stores. That's another secret shopping place that I have found nice professional clothes. If you're a person who would rather not wear "hand-me-downs", then those stores are not for you. But if you're on a budget, this is great information and you can always send your clothes to the cleaners before you wear them.

So how are you feeling? Feeling confident? Are you ready to show the world the new you? Not just yet, we have a little more learning to do. The next two chapters can be life changing if you pay attention and put the concepts into action! Next, we will cover "Beast Mode" the Job Fair!

LET'S GO!

Lesson 8 Review Notes

Lesson 9
"BEAST MODE"
THE JOB FAIR

"Unfortunately, there seems to be far more opportunity out there than ability... We should remember that good fortune often happens when opportunity meets with preparation."

~ Thomas A. Edison

I chose to title this chapter "Beast Mode" the Job Fair, of course referring to the great Marshawn Lynch, a NFL running back (referencing Seattle Seahawk years). Let me explain why. Before Marshawn Lynch faced a new opponent, he studied every defensive player, knew which players that were targeting to tackle his legs, knew which players had poor tackling skills, and knew which players that would be easier for him to attack. So when the game came, he was very confident because he knew he was prepared and all he had to do was be patient, so that whenever he gets the opportunity to expose the oppositions weaknesses, he would do it in BEASTY way!

The underlying theme of that whole message is to be prepared to be astonishing at the job fair! There are plenty of people who get opportunities to do something great or display their skills, but they are not prepared for it. I know that some people approach job fairs with doubt, thinking about how many other people are going to be there, the level of competition, etc. The key is to be prepared, period!

Below, I will share with you the six tips I have obtained to be a standout at a job fair.

Tip #1: Be prepared to: be **PATIENT**; wait in lines; be energetic; network; give your elevator speech; impress recruiters; get an interview!

Tip #2: Whenever you find out there's a job fair you should seek out the list of companies that are coming so that you can narrow down on a few companies that you know are hiring for a specific job that you are interested in.

Tip #3: With that knowledge, you can get information on those specific companies, and tweak your resume for those specific jobs as we discussed earlier.

Tip #4: Be prepared to speak on your resume when the time comes to talk to the recruiter. Approach the recruiter with a firm handshake and a graceful smile. Make sure your 60/90 second elevator speech is well rehearsed and precise! This is the time to be sharp and impressive!

Tip #5: Be sure to ask the recruiter for their contact information as well (email), so that you can properly follow up with them. They talk to a minimum of a hundred students per day, so you have to do everything you can to put yourself in a position to make the difference.

Tip #6: Also remember: dress for success (Business Attire); have business cards; no chewing gum; no earrings (men) and no excessive nose or lip rings.

If you follow these techniques, surely you will leave confident knowing that you gave your all! Now all you have to do is properly follow up with them, and everything will happen as planned.

The next chapter, we will discuss mastering the interview.

Lesson 9 Review Notes

Lesson 10
MASTERING THE INTERVIEW

"When you leave college, there are thousands of people out there with the same degree you have; when you get a job, there will be thousands of people doing what you want to do for a living. But you are the only person alive who has sole custody of your life."

~Anna Quindlen

If you can master the interview, you can get any job that you set yourself up for. This is where you put all of the learnings from the previous chapters together, with the additional knowledge you'll gain from this chapter, and show off your skills! This chapter will give you the key to the behavioral interview process, face to face interview tips, and how to close an interview.

Behavioral Interviewing

What is behavioral interviewing? Behavioral based interviewing is interviewing based on discovering how the interviewee acted in specific employment-related situations. The logic is that how you behaved in the past, will predict how you will behave in the future.

In a traditional interview, you will be asked a series of questions which typically have straight forward answers like "What are your strengths and weaknesses?" or "What major challenges and problems did you face? How did you handle them?" or "Describe a typical work week."

In a behavioral interview, an employer has decided what skills are needed in the person they hire and will ask questions to find out if the candidate has those skills. Instead of asking how you **would** behave, they will ask "how **DID** you behave." The interviewer will want to know how you handled a situation, instead of what you might do in the future.

Behavioral interview questions will be more pointed, more probing and more specific. For example:

Give an example of an occasion when you used logic to solve a problem.

Give an example of a goal you reached and tell me how you achieved it. Have you gone above and beyond the call of duty? If so, how?

What do you do when your schedule is interrupted? Give an example of how you handle it.

Have you had to convince a team to work on a project they weren't thrilled about? How did you do it?

Have you handled a difficult situation with a co-worker? How?

Tell me about how you worked effectively under pressure.

How to Answer Interview Questions:
Answer every question in terms of your background or qualifications or in terms of the job to be filled.

"Tell me about yourself" means, "Tell me about your qualifications." Mention each job in terms of accomplishment or performance indicators.

Personality questions attempt to determine if you have qualities being sought. "What kind of manager are you?" Answer these questions in terms of the obvious answer supported by past or present experiences as proof of your claim.

Salary questions. When asked what you desire, say "I'm currently earning $_____. I am sure that you will make an offer that is fair and commensurate with my experience."

What's the best way to prepare? Since you don't know exactly what situations you will be asked about if it's a behavioral interview, refresh your memory and consider some special situations you have dealt with or projects you have worked on. You may be able to use them to help frame responses. Review the job description. You may be able to get a sense of what skills will be an asset from reading the job description and position requirements.

During the interview, if you are not sure how to answer the question, ask for clarification. Example: "Could you please repeat the question?" Then be sure to utilize the **STAR** response model, and include these points in your answer:

- The **S**ituation
- The **T**asks that needed to be done
- The **A**ction you took
- The **R**esults that happened

You can get an in-depth look at the STAR response and other techniques at https://www.livecareer.com/quintessential/star-interviewing. It's important to keep in mind that there are no right or wrong answers. The interviewer is simply trying to understand how you behaved in a given situation. How you respond will determine if there is a fit between your skills and the position the company is seeking to fill. So, listen carefully, be clear and detailed when you respond and, most importantly, be honest. If your answers aren't what the interviewer is looking for, this position may not be the best job for you anyway.

Face to Face Interview Tips

Tip #1: Be prepared! Preparation is the key to a successful interview. Review your resume/portfolio to make sure it's current and reflects your most successful accomplishments. Never go to an interview without researching the company first! Dress for success, which in this case that means business attire. Keep in mind the image you present should be highly professional and shows a success. Read through this guide the night before the interview.

Tip #2: Arrive early! You may have to fill out an application or additional forms. If you are delayed for any reason, notify the interviewer immediately. If you're late for the first interview, the company will get the impression that you may be late every day

Tip #3: Fill out all forms neatly and completely. Be accurate and never falsify any information.

Tip #4: Bring several extra copies of your resume.

Tip #5: Research all the information you can on the interviewer before the interview (Linked-In; Facebook; Twitter). You should know their name and impress them by having some knowledge of their background. Meet your interviewer with a smile and a firm handshake. Be friendly and pleasant. Speak clearly, directly, and politely. The object of the interview is to impress the employer with your personality as well as your qualifications, so he or she will offer you the job!

Tip #6: During the interview, keep a positive attitude. When answering questions, speak well of yourself, your experiences and your past supervisors. Your potential employer will want to know all about you, so give a brief, but complete, answers to the questions asked.

Tip #7: Ask the interviewer questions about the duties and responsibilities of the job. **Until the job is offered, don't ask about vacations, holidays, or fringe benefits.** Most companies offer competitive benefits, but you don't want to give the impression that your main concern is vacation time, rather than what contributions you plan to make with the company

Tip #8: Be aware of your manner as well as your words. Sit up straight and look the interviewer in the eye.

Don't let the following negative facts **cost you** the job:

- Poor personal appearance
- Being overly aggressive and overbearing
- Inability to express thoughts clearly-poor diction or grammar
- Lack of interest and enthusiasm
- Lack of confidence and poise
- Overemphasis on money and benefits
- Lack of maturity
- Criticism of past employers
- Failure to ask questions about the job
- Persistent attitude of "what can you do for me?"

Tip #9: Ask questions! Create a list and don't cross-examine. Make the questions job related and ask questions that require an explanation. For example:

Interest questions that pertain to job opportunity and the company.
(Example: Do your company participate in any charity events?)

Job satisfaction questions that pertain to the importance of job, responsibility, recognition and career growth.
(Example: How is performance measured in the role that I am pursuing?)

Past performance questions that concentrate on the people who previously held the position, their performance and where they are today.
(Example: What can I do to stand out as a leader?)

Online-Video Interviewing

With the technology we have today, there are employers that also choose to have interviews online with websites like Skype. With this type of interview, it is very important to make sure that you have a good internet connection, and that your background is clear and neat, with no distractions. If you must go to the library where it's quiet, do so! Make sure your phone is off and that you are ready 15 minutes ahead of schedule! I went through one video interview, allow me to share my experience. This interview applied a lot of pressure once I clicked the begin button. I clicked the begin button, and I was given 90 seconds to read and prepare for the first question. After the 90 seconds, the video recorder automatically started recording, and I was given three minutes to video record my answer. After it stopped, there was only one more re-try. Every question was set-up like that, which was very challenging. So if you come across one of these types of interviews, be prepared! A little trick I did was, use the first attempt to write down the question, then write out the answer as if I was recording it. This way on the one re-attempt I seemed a lot more prepared.

Closing the Interview

By the time it's time to close the interview, you have answered the two major questions uppermost in the interviewer's mind, which are:

Why are you interested in this company?
What can you offer?

At the close of the interview, summarize your qualifications, thank the interviewer for his or her time, and let the employer know you're interested in the position. Ask for the job or the next interview if the situation demands, by saying something like this:

"Mr. Doe, your company, its services and the people I've met are very impressive. I'm confident I could do an excellent job in the position we discussed. When can we schedule a second interview?" If you've made a great impression and feel that it is the correct time in the interview process, you could also ask "How soon might I be able to start?"

He or she will be impressed with your enthusiasm. If he or she makes the offer, then accept it if you're ready. If you'd like to think over the offer and discuss it with others, tell the employer that you need 24 hours and you'll get back to him or her the next day.

Don't be discouraged if no definite offer is made or no specific salary is discussed. The interviewer will probably want to communicate with others first or interview other candidates before making a decision. That's why you must prepare for the interview as if it's the only chance you'll have, because the next interviewer may be more qualified than you. It's mandatory to have a competitive mindset and put in extra effort into your preparation.

Now you're ready to get the career that you are seeking! The next chapter will cover the basis of financial literacy. I debated on including this chapter due to how broad the topic can be, but I know that just covering the basis for a student would be very helpful if they are unaware. So, let's move on to the next chapter so that you can be financially aware of the situations that will arise.

Lesson 10 Review Notes

Lesson 11
INTRO TO FINANCIAL LITERACY

"Financial literacy is an issue that should command our attention because many Americans are not adequately organizing finances for their education, healthcare, and retirement."

~ Ron Lewis

There are many "connotations" and definitions for financial literacy that I found while doing my research. I chose to highlight Investopedia, which according to them "Financial literacy is the possession of knowledge and understanding of financial matters. Financial literacy is mainly used in connection with personal finance matters. Financial literacy often entails the knowledge of properly making decisions about certain personal finance areas like real estate, insurance, investing, saving (especially for college), tax planning and retirement." As I told you in the previous chapter, financial literacy is very broad. As a student, I think it's most important to build your financial literacy knowledge around: understanding financial aid, student loan debt and its long-team effects, budgeting and saving. We will cover these below.

Getting financial aid can make it possible for you to go to college. Or it might enable you to attend a college you thought you couldn't afford. There are four main sources:
- Federal government (the largest source)
- State governments

- Colleges and universities
- Private organizations

One thing is for sure: If you don't fill out financial aid forms, you won't get any aid. Even if you think you may not qualify, you should still submit the forms. To qualify for many types of aid, you'll need to complete the Free Application for Federal Student Aid (FAFSA). This application gives you access to these types of aid:

Grants and scholarships: money you don't have to pay back

Work-study jobs: paid, part-time work that's generally on campus

Loans: money you need to pay back, usually after you graduate

The FAFSA qualifies you for federal aid, but many state governments and colleges also use this application to award their own aid. Complete the form online at www.fafsa.gov or download paper forms there. You can even import your family's tax information directly from the IRS website. Also, you may need a parent or guardian when filling this form out, because the form will need to calculate your EFC. The Expected Family Contribution, (EFC) is a measure of your family's financial strength and is calculated according to a formula established by law. Your family's taxed and untaxed income, assets, and benefits (such as unemployment or Social Security) are all considered in the formula. Also considered are your family size and the number of family members who will attend college during the year. The information you report on your Free Application for Federal Student Aid (FAFSA) or your *FAFSA4caster* is used to calculate your EFC. Schools use the EFC to determine your federal student aid eligibility and financial aid award. **Note:** Your EFC is **not** the amount of money your family will have to pay for college **nor** is it the amount of federal student aid you will receive. It is a number used by the school you're applying to, to calculate the amount of federal student aid you are eligible to receive.

Each college/university has its own unique school code, which can be found on your FAFSA application as well. Next, we'll cover student loan debt.

Student loan debt can be detrimental to life! This is most important because students that make their own financial decisions regarding loans may not understand that this is an investment in their future earnings that must be paid back. Some students will end up borrowing way more money than they need and find themselves repaying the government for the rest of their lives. It goes back to knowing how much money you want to make and the career that will satisfy your financial goal. You also need to understand that a student loan is a DEBT, which can and will affect your credit score. Nowadays, certain jobs look at credit scores and will base a hiring decision from that. Credit scores clearly show the financial decisions that you've made, whether they were good or poor decisions. We will cover some additional information regarding credit later in this section.

The last thing that I want to cover with you regarding student loans is over-payment checks. An overpayment check is exactly what it says, OVER paid, which means you had enough money to cover for the semester, so you now have the option to keep the money and owe it back later, or you can give it back if you don't need it. If the overpayment check is based on a scholarship, then great job! Scholarships and grants are money that you don't have to repay. If you're getting an overpayment check from a personal loan, make the best decision to know the interest rates and when you must start repaying the loan. The best advice I can give you is to apply for as many scholarships/grants that you can and seek out those work-study and student hourly jobs on campus! This will give you steady pay and its money that doesn't have to be paid back. I was one of the people that didn't know about overpayment checks until my sophomore year in college. When I learned how to get an overpayment check, I completely abused and misused it. What happens is you get so caught up with other students poorly using their overpayment check on

Jordan's, clothes and other miscellaneous items, that you find yourself doing the same thing and not thinking with the end in mind. So many students, like myself, were buying cars and jewelry and not thinking about all the debt we were building. That's why I am stressing these facts to you so that you don't have to travel down that rode like I did, completely blind to the facts. I also suggest that you seek out the work-study jobs that are related to your specific career field. Mainly because you can build up experience and build relationships with others in your industry/field. You have to seek out these jobs early because they will go fast. Also, just to clarify, work-study jobs are jobs that you get an approved financial budget for a semester, through applying for financial aid. So, if you're awarded $3,500 in work-study, once you have worked enough hours to satisfy that amount your job will end. Student-hourly jobs, on the other hand, are jobs that the department has a separate budget for your wages. Which means you'd be able to work throughout the semester with no problems, unless their budget runs out which is rare in a single semester. Next let's discuss budgeting and saving.

Budgeting and saving are skills that must become a habit! Most people have never had to do this until they get out on their own and start paying monthly reoccurring bills, which is when they get to learn hands on. For you to get ahead of the curve, I recommend that you make a personal income and balance sheet (If you are not familiar with these financial statements, the terminology can be found on google.com). This will show in detail the income you have coming in and out (bills), and the money that you have tied up in savings or investments. This is one of the hardest things to do if you're not used to doing it, but once perfected, you will have a grip on each penny that's going out of your wallet. It's also a great idea to start saving a little money here and there, for what I like to call emergency funds. These emergencies are the situations that rarely and randomly happens but are costly. For example, your car engine goes bad, and your insurance doesn't cover parts and labor, or a random death to someone that's close to you, and you have to fly out or maybe help out with the financial obligations because the person wasn't insured. There are numerous types of emergencies that I'm sure you are thinking about now, so it's best to have some emergency funds! The worst thing that could happen is not having the funds and now you have to TRY and make your emergency someone else's emergency which doesn't always work out how we plan. By starting to save and budget now, you'll allow yourself to get ahead of the curve and not set yourself up for failure while adapting some financial principles. The last few items we're going to cover are: Assets Vs, Liabilities, Income, Banking, and Credit.

Assets Vs. Liabilities:

This information regarding assets and liabilities are very important no matter what industry you are in! As a student, this is very important because some people have student loan debt which they may not account for from a long-term perspective. This information is also important because many people are never taught this information, and grow to believe that certain expenses are assets. For example: jewelry, cars, Jordan's, or a house that you're renting. If you buy a car from the car lot, it loses around 10% of its value in the first month, also majority of jewelry can't be sold for the same price that you buy it for. This is called **depreciation**. **Appreciation** is an increase in the value of an asset over time.

Assets increase your wealth, while liabilities cost you money. Assets create or preserve wealth, making them extremely important to both individuals and companies. Robert Kiyosaki, author of Rich Dad Poor Dad, concludes that what makes the rich richer and the poor poorer is that the rich spend their money on assets, while the poor waste their money on liabilities, which they think of as assets. Let's examine how asset work on a balance sheet.

Common asset categories include cash and cash equivalents; accounts receivable; inventory; prepaid expenses; and property and equipment.

Although physical assets commonly come to mind when one thinks of assets, not all assets are tangible. Trademarks and patents are examples of intangible assets.

Assets are presented on the balance sheet in order of their liquidity. Current assets, which are expected to be consumed or converted to cash within one year, are listed at the top. Cash, short-term investments and inventory are examples of current assets.

Long-term assets, or fixed assets, are expected to be consumed or converted to cash after one year's time, and they are listed on the balance sheet beneath current assets. Property (such as office space or buildings) and equipment are common long-term assets.

Investors buy assets with the understanding that assets should hold, or even better, grow their economic value over time. Common asset classes for individual investors include stocks, bonds, cash, foreign currencies, collectibles, precious metals, real estate and commodities. A collection of assets is called a "portfolio," and it is widely believed that an individual's portfolio should include assets from several different categories, a process called "asset allocation."

Liabilities are legal obligations or debt owed to another person or company. In other words, liabilities are future sacrifices of economic benefits that an entity is required to make to other entities as a result of past events or past transactions.

Defined by the International Financial Reporting Standards (IFRS) Framework: "A liability is a present obligation of the enterprise arising from past events, the settlement of which is expected to result in an outflow from the enterprise of resources embodying economic benefits."

There are three main classifications of liabilities:

Current liabilities (short-term liabilities) are liabilities that are due and payable within one year.

Non-current liabilities (long-term liabilities) are liabilities that are due after a year or more.

Contingent liabilities are liabilities that may or may not arise depending on a certain event.

Current liabilities, also known as short-term liabilities, are debts or obligations that need to be repaid within a year.

Examples of Current Liabilities:
Accounts payable
Interest payable
Income taxes payable
Bills payable
Bank account overdrafts
Accrued expenses
Short-term loans

Non-current liabilities, also known as long-term liabilities, are debts or obligations that are due in over a year's time.

Examples of Non-Current liabilities:
Bonds payable
Long-term notes payable
Deferred tax liabilities
Mortgage payable
Capital lease

Contingent liabilities are liabilities that may occur depending on the outcome of a future event. Therefore, contingent liabilities are potential liabilities. For example, when a company is facing a lawsuit of $100,000, the company would face a liability if the lawsuit proves successful.

Examples of Contingent liabilities:
Lawsuits
Product warranties

Next, we'll cover gross income and net income which is great information for anyone.

If you're looking for a job or doing any type of work that gives you a real paycheck, you must think about gross income vs. net income.

Gross income: is the amount of salary or wages paid to the individual by an employer, before any deductions are taken

Net income: is the remaining amount of earnings after all deductions have been taken such as payroll taxes and retirement plan contributions.

It's very important to know that taxes and deductions will be taken out of every check, and the cost will vary in every state. Not to mention, if you have medical, dental and vision insurances taken out of your check, this will change the net income (take home money) as well.

Banking:

With a bank account, you get a statement that can be referred to whenever you like. Cash that is hidden at home never earns interest, but savings in a bank account do, so your money grows over time. The amount of interest you earn on money in your saving account will depend a lot on these 3 factors.

- The interest rate

- How long you keep the money in your account
- Rate the financial institution pays interest

Interest earned vs. Interest paid

Interest earned: When you deposit money at the bank, you may earn interest on that money -- especially in savings accounts or certificates of deposit (CDs).

In a sense, you're lending money to the bank so they can use it elsewhere. In return, you get interested income. **Interest paid** is the cost of borrowing money. Interest rates are normally expressed as % of the total borrowed. The Annual cost of a loan to a borrower including fees like interest rate. APR is expressed as a percentage.

Credit

The Credit Bureau is an agency that researches and collects individual credit information and sells it for a fee to creditors so they can decide on granting loans. Credit bureaus will look at an individual's borrowing and bill-paying habits to determine whether they represent a risky loan.

Tips for building good credit:

- Always pay bills on time, so you do not establish yourself as a 'late' payer.
- Set up automatic payments with your credit card company and bank:
- Always pay the monthly minimum or risk a penalty.
- Register to pay the balance on the credit card.
- Register to pay a set amount every month.

- Remember charging a credit card is essentially like taking out a loan

Tips to keep good credit:

- Don't write a check for more money you don't have in your account
- Pay your bills in full and on time
- Always keep your promises to repay the money you borrow
- Avoid having a credit card debt that exceeds 10% of monthly net income
- Never borrow more than 10% of your annual income.
- Avoid overdraft fees: (Automatic overdraft by overdrawing their account)

Now, you are ready to be all that you can be! Remember, you have to begin with the END in mind, first! Even with this book, you'll start making financial decisions before you get an interview for a job, so you must keep financial literacy as a primary principle. Also, do more research on financial literacy. As I told you, this topic is very broad, and there are things I didn't cover like: real estate, tax planning, retirement, and stocks and bonds. My goal was to make sure you understand the basis from a student standpoint, and the troubles that I faced that got me behind in life.

Now that you have all this information and are aware of the different challenges that will arise **IT'S ON YOU**! You have to decide to apply it! No one is going to do that for you; it's all up to you! My life is a testimony that it does not matter where you are from, whether you had parents or where you started. You must decide at some point and time in your life to introduce your dreams to execution if not your dreams will only be a thought. Also, it's okay to dream big, but you must make sure that your grind matches the level of success you want to reach. Don't get discouraged by someone else telling you that you can't do it, or it's not right, just stay on course and trust the process. The truth is they don't believe because they don't see YOUR end goal! So let's focus on having a tunnel vision for success, and everything will happen like it's supposed to!

Thank you for investing time to utilize this workbook, allowing me to pour my knowledge into you. I believe in you, and I know that you will be a success! Let your pain, fuel your passion, to fulfill your purpose! I look forward to hearing about your legacy!

Lesson 11 Review Notes

BONUS MATERIAL
The Power of Mentorship

"Do I Pick or Choose a Mentor?"

Knowing how to pick or choose a mentor is a necessity! But really, what is a mentor? Some people get confused between having a mentor vs. having a role model. I must say that there is a difference. A mentor knows you and cares about you and tries to help you succeed. You have an actual two-way relationship with a mentor. A role model is simply a person you look up to and try to be like. If I had to sum it up, I would say that a mentor is:

- An advisor, who has career interests similar to the career you want to pursue and shares knowledge with you formally or informally.

- A supporter, who gives the necessary level of emotional and moral encouragement, as, for example, prior to a major test or challenge you're facing.

- A sponsor, who provides sources of information about research, grant, internships, employment, or other opportunities.

- A tutor, who gives specific, timely, and constructive feedback on performance.

- A model, who is a professional with integrity, thereby serving as a good role model.

There are many things to keep in mind when selecting a mentor, from your needs to the mentor's availability. The first step I'd like to address is, you must be aware that you need a mentor and what you need a mentor for. You wouldn't typically need a mentor to hear your funny jokes, that would be a waste of both of your times. Next, I will share some strategies to assist you through your mentor selection process.

Selecting a Mentor

- Get a feel for your prospective mentors by enrolling in their courses (if they teach) and asking your fellow students about their mentoring experiences with these/this person(s). You want to be sure that you will be comfortable working with this person and are receptive to his or her mentoring style.

- Confirm that your prospective mentor has current interests that complement your own.

- Ask about your prospective mentor's ability to provide resources (time, funding, etc.) To support your research and goals.

- Consider your prospective mentor's academic rank, tenure status, current mentoring load, and connections with individuals in the types of jobs you'd like after graduation.

Working with a Mentor

- Start your mentoring relationship on a positive note by being open and honest from the beginning.

- Let your mentor know how your previous experiences (academic, professional, or personal) are in line with his/her interests.

- Make a plan for how often you'll meet with your mentor and how best to contact your mentor with questions outside your scheduled meeting times. (Skype, in-person, etc.)

- Be respectful of your mentor's time. Always arrive at meetings on time and be prepared for meetings with notes from previous meetings, a list of discussion points, and a summary of the work you've done since your last meeting.

- Keep in contact with your mentor even when your research progress is slow. Communicate regularly and always ask questions when they arise.

Different Mentors, Different Roles

Your primary research mentor may not be able to meet all your needs in a mentoring relationship. Consider seeking multiple mentors who can give you guidance and advice in other areas. I suggest a:

- Professional mentor: for career/entrepreneurship advice.

- Personal mentor: to assist with day-to-day personal development, someone you can see regularly.

- Peer mentor: someone in your age range that you see regularly, that will hold you accountable daily and strives to be great themselves.

- Financial mentor: someone to give you advice and raise your awareness about strategically investing, saving money & raising money, and retirement.

If you're in school, a teacher can help you develop skills through observing and evaluating your performance in the classroom. He or she may also be able to help you find opportunities to further strengthen your weaknesses.

Your career mentor can also discuss your career goals and give you advice on professional development. Ask your mentor to introduce you to individuals (colleagues, potential employers, other professionals) who may be able to help you advance your career. A career mentor can also help you hone your interviewing skills and prepare you for negotiating your first contract.

Finally, keep in touch with your mentors. They'll want to know about your successes and may be able to continue to provide professional and career advice.

It's your responsibility to actively seek mentors to support your work and enhance your graduate education. Carefully select mentors that share your interest and can meet your needs, and build relationships based on honesty and trust. Your mentoring relationships will likely continue beyond your graduate education, and you'll benefit from academic, professional, and personal mentoring relationships that help you become a professional who can, in turn, mentor others.

The Power of Mentorship Review Notes

BONUS MATERIAL
The Entrepreneur in You

There's a little bit of an entrepreneur in everyone, it just depends on whether you decide to tap into it or not. In my eyes, entrepreneurship is a major key, to financial freedom and creating generational wealth. I'm not saying this to say that a person can't create generational wealth or reach financial freedom by working for someone else, but the one benefits that being an entrepreneur provides, is the ability to fire yourself on your own terms. Not someone else's. I've worked many jobs in my lifetime, and the reason I'm so passionate about entrepreneurship is because of two personal experiences I had working for two different companies. The first time I was terminated, I knew that it was going to happen before it happened. Not because I had an inside connection, but because I was fed up with the way I was being treated and I was going to terminate them soon! Because of the preliminary tensions that I felt, I started writing my first book during my lunchbreaks, preparing for the next phase of my life. This eventually led me to the thought and reality of becoming an author and speaker. The second time, I was terminated for doing the job that was given to me. Sounds crazy right!? It is crazy, but I know that everything happens for a reason. Being terminated unexpectedly, led me to discover the resilient me, a true lion heart. I found a different level of passion for what I was doing! My back was against the wall, and I was forced to go all in with my business aggressively. Now you should have a deeper understanding of why this book, and my passion for education and entrepreneurship are so real.

To be an entrepreneur requires ambition, determination, discipline and a resilient mentality. Speaking from experience, all these characteristics are necessary! There will be times that you will get side tracked, fail projects, miss deadlines and other things. You may also experience not having enough money to fund your idea. The most important fact that you must understand, is each problem or issue that you face, should be a learning experience for you to grow and get better from. Not to mention, life and death will still occur in the most random moments, so you must instill resiliency into your daily diet. In the lowest points of your mood and life, you must find and remember your WHY?! You must remind yourself why you're doing what you're doing, who you're doing it for and how it's going to enhance the life for the generation after you. This kind of goes back to lesson one, developing a mindset to create generational wealth. Your mindset will assist you to get past hardships, no matter the situation, stay dedicated and determined! YOU ARE RESILIENT!!

Let's get down to the nitty gritty! If you don't have the family structure to support you financially to start a business it's going to be tuff, period! This means you must find ways to raise money and find sponsors/donors. It can be difficult, but it can be accomplished. There are a several routes that you can take to become an entrepreneur, I will only highlight one way to do it with technology and social media. Lastly, I will provide seven basic steps to start a business.

How to Start an E-commerce Business Using Social Media

In less than twenty years, social media has revolutionized not only our communication culture but how we conduct business. The dizzying effect of unfettered and unlimited 24-hour access to people and information has transformed the various tools into a game changer. There is a broad and increasing list of sites, including BlinkList, YouTube, Delicious, Instagram, Pinterest, Flickr, Tumblr, BlogMarks.net, and the triumvirate of major sites: Twitter, Facebook, and LinkedIn. These social destinations have become to business professionals and entrepreneurs, opportunity to strategically network and close deals based on shared interests and personal engagement. But these sites do more, by offering users valuable real estate to advertise products or services, create and expand brand recognition, solicit feedback, build relationships, and create community forums. Users also have unprecedented access to consumers, hiring managers, prospective clients, industry experts, and opportunities.

Also, social media levels the playing field by allowing anyone access without restrictions on time, location, or social status. The most diligent and creative players are reaping huge benefits. According to a recent Nielsen research says Americans spend nearly 25% of their time online on social networks and blogs, up from nearly 16% a year ago. The initial foray into social media can be daunting and bewildering. Newcomers to the space might wonder: Who's reading? Will I be heard or noticed? Isn't it all just fun and games? Isn't it invasive? Making an effort worthwhile requires time, patience, and a work-smart-not-hard strategy. Whether you're an entrepreneur or a corporate professional, the success of marketing your products, businesses, or your brand will be determined by how well you engage interest on the varying platforms. Here, I will offer you some tips to get you connected.

What Upcoming Business Owners Should Know

Finding out who your customers are and how they like to be served is essential for the success of any business. Questions and surveys offered on social media platforms can help business owners quickly access that information. Such data can help you position your product to broader groups outside your initial base of contacts. Put your product in front of the trendsetters or the next level of users. Targeted searches let you drill down beneath the surface to find followers and potential influencers that can use or promote your product or service."

Location-based social mapping services such as Foursquare, Google Latitude, Loopt, Facebook Places, and MyTown, allow consumers to benefit from their influence. For example, if you visit your favorite flower shop in Tucson and tweet it to your followers, you get $2 off your purchase. The higher the network and influence, the bigger the discount. These services also enable users to find friends and events; share locations, updates, tips, photos, and comments; and share across online social networks and blogs. Google Latitude and Foursquare boast more than 10 million users each. Greater social media interactivity has been facilitated by mobile apps such as Facebook, Telegram, and Whatsapp. According to a Juniper Research report, the number of downloads from mobile application stores is expected to rise from fewer than 25 billion per year in 2015 to more than 100 billion in 2035.

How to Maximize Social Media Marketing to Promote Your Brand or Business

A blogging platform such as WordPress or Blogspot is essential, and Twitter, etc. Blogs have greater potential for organic leads because their content-rich nature makes them more search engine friendly. Search engines love content-driven platforms and rank them higher than static websites. Think of your blog as a launch pad or hub for your enterprise. Your social media efforts should lead back to your blog or website, which should be dynamic and informative, providing content and information that encourages visitors not only to return but to distribute your content to their network. Blogs or websites should contain SEO, or search engine optimized, keywords and phrases that help visitors find the business when they search via Google, Yahoo, Bing, and others. Ensure to pull in RSS feeds and useful links into your blog. RSS feeds allow you to import content from outside sources and are a great way to share information that visitors find interesting. You should also work on engagement and consistency. For example, your Twitter timeline should be a combination of original updates, retweets, or shares from other sources, replies from connections, inspirational quotes, and trending topics. A standard formula is two to four tweets per day. Positive activity can also blossom quickly and create a buzz that reaches well beyond a business' core audience. In the virtual world, consumers and job seekers can become influencers and trendsetters by persuading their network to take action or buy a product or service. Next, choose a picture for your social media avatar, rather than a logo. People like faces associated with companies. Customize your Twitter background. Use photos, links, contact information, RSS feeds, etc. to individualize and promote your brand. You can also choose a third-party application or service, such as TweetDeck or Hoot Suite, SocialOomph and Twaitter, which allows quick, easy distribution of posts and other content among multiple social media sites. You can incorporate plug-ins or apps on the sidebar of your blog page that allows visitors to access all your social media easily. All social media sites have plug-ins or widgets that allow fast, easy updates with one click.

Remember, don't follow everyone who follows you on Twitter. Conduct targeted keyword searches for individuals, companies, and other industry players who are important to you or who you want to have as a client. Also, show off your expertise. If you're in business, you're already an expert with valuable information people want to know. Use your talents, passion, ability, and personality to your advantage.

Now that you are aware of how you can use social media to start a business, next we will cover how to file your business. Below are 7 steps that you can take to start a business.

Step 1. Decide on a Legal Structure

The most common legal structures for a small business are:
- sole proprietorship
- partnership
- limited liability company (LLC), and

- corporation

There also are special versions of some of these structures, such as limited partnerships and S corporations. You'll want to consider which business entity structure offers the type of liability protection you want and the best tax, financing, and financial benefits for you and your business. Google: Choose on Nolo's website for more information on how to choose the best ownership structure for your business.

Step 2. Choose a Name

For LLCs and corporations, you will need to check that your name is distinguishable from the names of other business entities already on file with the Texas Secretary of State (SOS). You can check for available names by doing a name search on the SOS direct website (use google). You can reserve an available name for 120 days by filing an application for reservation or renewal of reservation of an entity name form with the Texas SOS. There are certain name requirements for LLCs and corporations (like including a word such as "LLC" for LLCs or "Company" for corporations). Google **How to Form an LLC** in Texas and **How to Form a Corporation** in Texas for more information.

If your business is a sole proprietorship or partnership that uses a business name that is different from the name of the business owner (for a sole proprietorship) or names of the individual partners (for a partnership)? If so, you must register an assumed business name with the county clerk in the county where you will do business.

If you plan on doing business online, you may want to register your business name as a domain name. Google **Choose and Register a Domain Name** for more information. In addition, to avoid trademark infringement issues, you should do a federal and state trademark check to make sure the name you want to use is not the same as or too similar to a name already in use. Google **How to Do a Trademark Search** for more information.

Step 3. Create Your Business Entity

Sole proprietorship: To establish a sole proprietorship in Texas, you don't need to file any organizational documents with the state. For more information, google **How to Establish a Sole Proprietorship** in whichever state you live.

Partnership: To create a general partnership in Texas, you don't need to file any organizational documents with the state. Although not legally required, all partnerships should have a written partnership agreement. The partnership agreement can be very helpful if there is ever a dispute among the partners. For more information, google **How to Form a Partnership in Texas**. To form a limited liability partnership (often used by professionals), you must file a Registration with the Texas SOS. For more information, google **How to Form a Limited Liability Partnership in Texas**.

LLCs: To create an LLC in Texas, you must file a **Certificate of Formation** with the Texas SOS. You will also need to appoint a registered agent in Texas for service of process. In addition, while not required by law, you also should prepare an operating agreement to establish the basic rules about how your LLC will operate. The operating agreement is not filed with the state. For more information, see **How to Form an LLC in Texas** and **How to Form a Professional LLC in Texas** (for professionals).

Corporations: To create a corporation in Texas, you must file a **Certificate of Formation** with the Texas SOS. You will also need to appoint a registered agent in Texas for service of process. Although not legally required, you also should prepare bylaws to establish your corporation's internal operating rules. Bylaws are not filed with the state. S Corporations must also file IRS Form 2553, **Election by a Small**

Business Corporation, with the IRS. For more information, google **How to Form a Corporation in Texas.**

Step 4. Licenses and Permits

Firstly, **tax registration.** If you will be selling goods in Texas, you must apply for a sales tax permit with the Comptroller of Public Accounts (CPA). More generally, any business operating in Texas should register with the CPA. You can register online or on paper. If your business has employees or is taxed separately from you, you must obtain a federal Employer Identification Number (EIN) from the IRS. Even if you are not required to obtain an EIN, there are often business reasons for doing so. Banks often require an EIN to open an account in the business's name and other companies you do business with may require an EIN to process payments. You can get an EIN by completing an online application on the IRS website. There is no filing fee. Regulatory licenses and permits. These cover areas such as:

- Health and safety
- The environment
- Building and construction; and
- Specific industries or services.

You can find guidance on state licenses and permit from the SOS **Guides and Resources** webpage (use google). Many business licenses and permits in Texas are issued at the city or county level. For information about these local licenses and permits, check the websites for any cities or counties where you will do business.

Let's cover professional and occupational licenses. These cover people who work in various fields. The Texas Department of Licensing and Regulation handles licensing for a certain specialized professions and industries. Businesses that provide professional services generally must apply for a Certificate of Authority through the Secretary of State. You can file the application through the SOS Direct website (google).

Step 5. Business Location and Zoning

You'll need to pick a location for your business and check local zoning regulations. That includes if you work from home. You may be able to find zoning regulations for your town or city by googling municode.com.

Step 6. Taxes and Reporting

Because Texas does not have a personal income tax, owners of some forms of business will not owe state tax on their business income. Google **Texas State Business Income Tax** for more information on state business taxes in Texas. Next, sole proprietorships. Sole proprietors pay federal taxes on business income as part of their personal federal income tax returns. Partnerships pay federal taxes on partnership income. In addition, most Texas partnerships are subject to the state's franchise tax, but only owe the tax if total revenue exceeds a certain amount. Limited liability partnerships (LLPs) and certain limited partnerships (LPs) must file an annual report with the SOS. LLC Members pay federal taxes on their share of LLC income on federal tax returns. LLCs themselves are subject to the state's franchise tax, but only owe the tax if total revenue exceeds a certain amount. Unlike other states, Texas does not require LLCs to file an annual report. Google **Texas LLC Annual Report and Tax Requirements** for more information. With corporations, a shareholder-employee with a salary must pay federal income tax on his or her personal federal tax return. The corporation itself is subject to the state's franchise tax. Apart from Texas taxes, there are federal income and employer taxes. Google IRS Publications 334, Tax Guide for Small Business.

Step 7. Insurance

Insurance is a good idea for most kinds of business. While insurance often is regulated at the state level, the types of business insurance available are usually similar across the fifty states. Google **Obtaining Business Insurance** for more information.

Follow these steps and you will be well on your way to entrepreneurship. If you are not located in Texas, be sure to google whichever city or state you are in. I hope that you find this information valuable and that you put it to use! I'm sure I will see you at the top! Don't meet me there, **BEAT ME THERE!**

The Entrepreneur in You Review Notes

Sterling Mark, M.B.A.

ACADEMIC GRIND

Written by: Sterling Mark

My people, my people……. I really need your attention,

Not to look at Instagram or snapchat, but there's a critical issue regarding our retention;

I need you right now because, I don't want it to be too late,

Not only is there a problem with our retention, but we have a staggeringly low graduation rate;

There's a disconnect making the collegiate transition, and it's causing us to waste so much time,

If only we knew how to seek the knowledge that we needed, and begin with the end, in mind;

We live in an era now where people love to give social media their all,

Completely blind to the fact that a pic or a post, could be your career downfall;

It's time to regain our focus and take complete control of our lives,

We need to instill true grit within ourselves, and assure that we understand, the whys;

Like, why are you here? And who all are depending on you to succeed?

With that realization, you can create a better future for your family and build an empire for your seeds;

Look deep inside yourself, find your purpose within your passion,

Passion combined with purpose, will make your relevance, everlasting;

And as you gradually take steps forward, to position yourself for greatness,

Understand, there will be hard times ahead, but it is then that you can recollect this information;

As we all know, information, that changes situations,

And knowledge is the new money, so it's imperative to have a higher education;

So get it together right now, and get on your academic grind,

Tomorrow is never promised, so now is the time!!!

RESOURCE PAGE

Testing resources for 3rd-12th grade students & incoming college freshman students in Texas:

http://www.collegeforalltexans.com/index.cfm?objectid=C5B9B2F7-CEFE-0E2F-2464BF8E0EFDF5E0 (STAAR, SAT, ACT)

http://www.collegeforalltexans.com/index.cfm?objectid=63176344-FFFA-217B-60C9A0E86629B3CA (Incoming College Students; TSI information)

https://www.topuniversities.com/student-info/admissions-advice/graduate-admissions-tests-glance-gmat-gre-lsat-toefl-ielts (Graduate School Test: GMAT, GRE, LSAT, TOEFL, IELTS)

Financial Aid, Scholarship and College Resources:

http://www.collegeforalltexans.com/index.cfm?objectid=699B6A67-A725-CF93-E4BE5B7F74474508

www.fafsa.ed.gov
Learn all about the Free Application for Federal Student Aid, which is usually the first step in seeking financial aid for higher education.

https://studentaid.ed.gov/sa/
The Department of Education's Federal Student Aid programs is the largest source of student aid in America. These programs provide more than $80 billion a year in grants, loans, and work-study assistance. Learn more about and how to apply for this aid.

www.fastweb.com
FastWeb is a free scholarship search service that can help students find need-based and merit assistance as well as jobs and internships.

www.nasfaa.org
The National Association of Student Financial Aid Administrators offers a range of resources to help students, parents, and counselors navigate the college aid process.

CollegeBoard.org
While the College Board is known for its college-readiness tests, it also has an arm that focuses on scholarships. Big Future hosts scholarships, as well as other financial aid and internship information from more than 2,200 programs — totaling nearly $6 billion. In order to get the most accurate search results, it's critical to fill out as many details as you can in the profile that's used for searching.

Niche.com
Formerly known as College Prowler, Niche is a great tool that can help you find colleges AND money. It's organized into categories that make it pretty easy to find what you're looking for — allowing users to search by interest, career, major and other areas.

Scholarship Monkey
Scholarship Monkey allows you to search for scholarships a few different ways. You can search by keyword, browse scholarship lists (various categories/topics) and also see lists of the latest and featured scholarships. The site also allows you to create a personal profile for more accurate results.

Cappex
Cappex hosts a database of more than $11 billion in scholarship opportunities. Once you create a personal profile, you can search for opportunities that directly match your strengths and skills. Plus, Cappex has a tool that will calculate your odds of getting into a certain college before you even apply.

Chegg
Chegg is widely known for its online textbook store that allows students to either rent or buy textbooks for cheap. But Chegg is also a great resource for finding scholarships — more than $1 billion worth of them.

To search for available scholarships, click on the menu stack at the top right of the homepage and select the "scholarships" in the drop-down menu. Once you create a personal profile, you can search for available opportunities that match your criteria. Chegg also has a "top scholarship picks this week" category that highlights some options you may have missed.

U.S. Labor Department's Free Search Tool
According to the official Student Aid website, this free tool is a great resource for

students to search more than 7,500 scholarships, grants and other various types of financial aid award opportunities.

The Career One Stop tool allows you to:
- Look through the site's entire inventory of scholarships, arranged in order of closest deadline.
- Narrow your list with a "search by keyword" option: Just enter a keyword about the type of award you're looking for.
- Use the filters to see opportunities for only certain types of awards, locations, level of study, and more.

Unigo
Unigo hosts millions of available scholarships and makes it easy to search by type, including athletic scholarships, college-specific scholarships, company-based scholarships, minority scholarships, major-specific scholarships, state-specific scholarships and more. You can search by category or create a personal profile to get more specific results that match your needs. Unigo also offers scholarship contests and sweepstakes.

66 Minority College Scholarships for 2019 - Affordable Colleges Online
https://www.affordablecollegesonline.org/financial-aid-for-minorities/

Little Miss African American Scholarship Pageant: Founded in 1993 by Lisa Ruffin, this proram is based on the idea that young people must begin with a strong foundation. They believe that each of our girls possesses the promise of unlimited possibilities. Learn more at
www.scholarshipsonline.org/2018/06/little-miss-african-american-scholarship-pageant.html

Derrick Rose Scholars Program: Passionate about embodying a legacy that will empower the next generation to pursue greatness; NBA star Derrick Rose has launched a scholarship program called the Rose Scholars. The program is open to high school sophomore, junior + senior students who are civically minded and have an instinct to lead. Learn more at
www.scholarshipsonline.org/2018/08/derrick-rose-scholars-program.html

Beyonce's Homecoming Scholars Award Program: Beyoncé, through her BeyGOOD initiative, has established the Homecoming Scholars Award Program for students attending Xavier University, Wilberforce University, Tuskegee University and

Bethune-Cookman University – all Historically Black Colleges and Universities (HBCUs). Learn more at
www.scholarshipsonline.org/2018/04/beyonce-homecoming-scholars-award.html

National Hook-up of Black Women Scholarships: National Hook-up of Black Women (NHBW) Scholarships are available to graduating high school seniors who plan to enroll in an accredited college or university in the fall after graduation. Two different scholarships are available. Learn more at
www.scholarshipsonline.org/2017/02/national-hook-up-of-black-women-scholarships.html

The Bill Gates Scholarship For Minorities: a full tuition scholarship awarded to exceptional high school seniors planning to attend college full time. Applicants must be minorities, including African-American, American Indian/Alaska Native, Asian & Pacific Islander American, and/or Hispanic American. Learn more at
www.scholarshipsonline.org/2017/09/the-gates-scholarship.html

United Negro College Fund/ Michael Jackson Scholarship: The Michael Jackson scholarship provides financial assistance to communication arts and social science students attending a UNCF college/university during the current academic year. Candidates must have a minimum GPA of 2.5 on a 4.0 scale. Learn more at
www.scholarshipsonline.org/2015/05/michael-jackson-uncf-scholarship.html

Costco Scholarship Fund For Minority Students: Costco Scholarship Fund is open to underrepresented minority students who are planning to attend either the University of Washington or Seattle University. The fund was established to provide qualified minority students access to education benefits. Scholarship awards are based on financial need. Learn more at
www.scholarshipsonline.org/2014/10/costco-scholarship-fund.html

Coca-Cola Scholars Program: a very competitive program for high school seniors throughout the United States. Sponsored by The Coca-Cola Company, the largest soft drink company in the world, the program awards millions every year in college funding. Learn more at
www.scholarshipsonline.org/2012/04/coca-cola-scholars-program.html

Jill Scott's Blues Babe Foundation Scholarship Program: The Blues Babe Foundation Scholarship Program is open to current undergraduate students who are pursuing careers in the writing arts. The program was created by three-time GRAMMY award-winning singer-songwriter Jill Scott. Learn more at

www.scholarshipsonline.org/2015/09/mahogany-blues-babe-foundation.html

Generation Google Scholarship For Underrepresented Students in Technology: Founded in 1993 by Lisa Ruffin, this program is based on the idea that young people must begin with a strong foundation. They believe that each of our girls possesses the promise of unlimited possibilities. Learn more at

www.scholarshipsonline.org/2013/11/generation-google-scholarship.html

Boeing/ Thurgood Marshall College Fund HBCU Scholarship Program: This program provides an unparalleled career opportunity and scholarship for outstanding students attending Boeing HBCU priority schools. High performing students currently in their sophomore year, with a minimum GPA of 3.3 are encouraged to apply. Learn more at

www.scholarshipsonline.org/2018/08/boeing-thurgood-marshall-college-fund-hbcu-scholarship.html

GLOSSARY

Asset: Something valuable that an entity owns, benefits from, or has use of, in generating income

Liabilities: A claim against the assets, or legal obligations of a person or organization, arising out of past or current transactions or actions. Liabilities require mandatory transfer of assets, or provision of services, at specified dates or in determinable future.

Overdraft fees: customers can incur an automatic overdraft by overdrawing their account by check, by atm, or by debit card at the point-of-sale. The study found that overdraft fees ranged from **$10** to **$38**, with a median fee of $27.

Saving accounts: usually an opening deposit is required to an account that you can that accrues interest over time that you can withdraw from a limited number of times per months based on the type of saving account you have.

Checking accounts: does not accrue interest allows for deposits to withdraw, write checks, use debit and atm cards and a varying balance

Deposits: a sum of money placed or kept in a bank account, usually to gain interest.

Apr: is the annual rate charged for borrowing or earned through investment, and is expressed as a percentage that represents the actual yearly cost of funds over the term of a loan.

Direct deposit: the electronic transfer of a payment directly from the account of the payer to the recipient's account.

Credit: the ability of a customer to obtain goods or services before payment, based on the trust that payment will be made in the future.

Loan: a thing that is borrowed, especially a sum of money that is expected to be paid back with interest.

Collection agencies: agency that collects debt for business to business and business to consumer

Credit bureaus: is a collection agency that gathers account information from various creditors and provides that information to a **consumer reporting agency**

Credit unions is a member-owned democratically controlled by its members, and operated to promote thrift, providing credit at competitive rates, and providing other financial services to its members.

Pre-approved loan: the lender's preliminary determination that a borrower would qualify for a particular **loan** amount under that lender's guidelines. The determination and **loan** amount is based on income and credit information.

College scholarship service (CSS) profile: The CSS profile is created and run by the College Board (the same people who bring you the lovely sat) to help provide more particulars about your financial situation. Though the FAFSA (see below) helps give colleges a general picture of your financial aid situation, the CSS profile can help fill in some gaps and provide more detailed information. The profile needs to be filled out at least two weeks before your first college or major scholarship deadline. It costs $25 to send the profile to one college and $16 to send it to every additional college.

One important thing to note is that while a CSS profile is not required by all schools, at least 350 different colleges use it, and the number of schools that ask for a CSS profile is growing every year.

Estimated cost of attendance (ECA): Your ECA describes how much it will cost you to attend your school (talk about scary!). Before you start exclaiming, "wait, can there be that many zeros in my tuition?!", Notice that it does say "cost of *attendance*," in that the number includes everything necessary for attending college: i.e., tuition, room and board, textbooks, traveling expenses, personal expenses, and a whole lot more. Obviously, all of these factors vary greatly from one person to another (for example, one person might only be traveling home twice per year, which can slash travel costs). Although this number might seem gigantic, it may not be how much you will pay, depending on your spending habits (hence, "estimated").

Estimated family contribution (EFC): The EFC is part of your student aid report (arguably the most crucial point), and it explains how much your family is expected to pay for your college education based on several financial factors, including taxed/untaxed income; your parents' jobs, assets and benefits; family size; and how many of your siblings are currently enrolled in college. Although the number is not set in stone, the idea of the EFC is to show how much money you should be receiving in aid (subtract your EFC from your EFC, and you'll get the amount of money you need from financial aid!).

Free application for federal student aid (FAFSA): The FAFSA is the basic financial aid application that every single person who desires college financial assistance must fill out (put a gigantic red circle around the word "must"!). It is used to determine how much you and your family can pay for your education. Filling out the FAFSA is beyond important to any college applicant's journey, as it is used for student loans and grants as well as for scholarships or financial aid packages given out by colleges.

Student aid report (SAR): After you submit your FAFSA, you will receive a student aid report that details the information you gave and how much money you and your family will be able to contribute to your college tuition. This report is jam-packed with information, including your all-important ECA and EFC. Your SAR will come anywhere from three to 10 days after you submit it, depending on if you fill out your FAFSA electronically or by mail.

Grants: Grants are funds that, unlike student loans, do not need to be repaid. They can come from federal or state governments, colleges, or other independent organizations. You can read more about federal and state grants offered to students on the U.S. Department of Education's federal student aid page.

Merit-based aid: Merit-based financial aid is given to students who meet certain academic or extracurricular requirements as set by an institution, group, or person. This can include a combination of GPA, test scores, and community involvement. An important note, pre-collegiate students: merit-based aid does not account for financial need, meaning that anyone with any type of financial background is eligible to obtain it!

Students can either apply for certain types of merit-based scholarships, or they can earn them automatically (for example, a university could give a certain amount of money to all applicants who have at least a 3.5 GPA or who have completed 100 community service hours).

Need-based aid: Need-based financial aid can come in the form of scholarships. As the name sounds, the main requirement for eligibility is a lack of financial assets. Every school has their system for determining what counts as "need" and in what areas, so definitely keep in close contact with your prospective schools' financial aid offices as the time gets closer to choosing a college!

Resilient: tending to recover from or adjust easily to misfortune or change.

Parent (plus) loans: Plus loans are federal loans granted to graduate students or parents of dependent undergraduate students who need additional financial aid. These loans come with a fixed interest rate of 7.9 percent, and your parents must have a good credit history. To find the maximum amount you can get for your plus loan, take your eca and subtract all other financial aid you've received.

Scholarships: The word "scholarship" covers a broad range of financial aid. Scholarships are considered "gift aid," so you don't have to pay them back. Many scholarships instruct the person receiving the award to use the funds towards a particular aspect of the college experience (textbooks, meal plans, etc.), but some provide finances for whatever part of college life the student needs the money for.

Are you looking to start your scholarship search? Some great websites to check out are fast web (which allows you to fill out a profile detailing your GPA, extracurricular, and interests and receive scholarship suggestions based on your data), scholarshipexperts.com (which also allows you to fill out a profile and keep track of scholarship deadlines), and zinc (which combines scholarship finding with the overall college admissions timeline).

Student loans: Student loans are given to college students to help them pay for tuition, living expenses, and other school-related means (like textbooks or lab equipment). What separates student loans from other types of loans is that they typically come with a deferred repayment schedule (i.e., the student starts paying off the loan after she graduates) and low-interest rates (between 3.4 and 6.8 percent).

Subsidized loans: Once your college reviews your FAFSA and determines that you have reason to receive need-based aid, there are two different types of loans you could receive: subsidized or unsubsidized loans. You may be given a subsidized loan, meaning (as mentioned above) that your interest rates are low (around 3.4 percent) and <u>you start paying them off after you graduate</u>.

<u>Unsubsidized loan:</u> Unsubsidized loans can be offered to anyone who submits a FAFSA profile. It is up to individual universities to decide how much money should be given to the student. Financial need is not necessary to receive one of these loans, and because of this fact, unsubsidized loans have a higher interest rate of 6.8 percent compared to their subsidized counterparts.

<u>Work-study:</u> Students participating in a work-study program are typically employed by their university (in a job at the campus store, the campus coffee shop, etc.) And have a certain amount of their wages donated to the student contribution of their financial aid. If you're looking at a work-study option, you will be negotiating with your school's financial aid office to figure out what your job will be, how much you'll earn per hour, and <u>how much of that income</u> will go towards your financial aid contribution. Don't worry that you won't be able to find a work-study job you like! Colleges offer tons of jobs for students, from working in the library to helping university communications with social media accounts (hint: colleges love students who know how to tweet effectively!) To being an usher for campus shows.

ABOUT THE AUTHOR

Mr. Mark is a proud and productive alumnus of Prairie View A&M University. He obtained a B.S. in Business Administration with a concentration in Marketing and a Master's degree in Business Administration (M.B.A.).

Mark's senior year, he worked as the Facility Supervisor at Recreational Sports at Prairie View A&M University. This was his first action of working with students hands-on in a supervisory role. Mark, managed over 30 student staff, which he led and directed to ensure safety and student development on a daily. He was also an active member of Collegiate 100, which initiated the transition for his astounding stalwart leadership that he was recognized for.

Upon completion of Mark's Bachelor's degree, life lessons showed him that education was the key. He applied and was accepted into the M.B.A. program at Prairie View, continuing his educational journey as well as his managerial role with Recreational Sports. During Mark's tenure with Rec-Sports, he pledged Alpha Phi Alpha Fraternity Incorporated Spring 2013. Mark is currently an avid and active leader within his chapter Epsilon Tau Lambda, which was awarded the Chapter of the Year Award. Mark has been recognized for his outstanding efforts and contributions within the chapter and is in the process of formulating a non-profit organization that aligns with Alpha's National Programs such as My Brother's Keeper and Project Alpha.

The summer of 2014, Mark was selected the 1st ever Vice President for Administration Intern at Prairie View A&M University. During his intern, he interacted with high-level executives daily, and led the initiative to bridge the gap between minorities graduating from a higher learning institution. Mark coordinated and conducted powerful weekly male success sessions, impacting the lives of over 90 incoming freshmen. He grabbed their attention with his dynamic narrative, then empowered them on how to matriculate through college struggles and gave real-life scenarios that they would face, demonstrating how to manage and resolve conflict in today's society. After reading the feedback from the student evaluations, it was clear that his purpose is to help minorities that come from hardships and make them aware of the many opportunities that college has to offer. This position was a life-changing experience for Mark, and it has opened the doors to many opportunities. Mark was invited to Washington D.C. for the White House Initiative on HBCU's, where he was able to network with influential people with similar interests in enhancing enrollment, retention and graduation rates among minorities. He also got invited to the Thurgood Marshall Leadership Institute, which is where he was able to land the job offer from Walmart.

Mr. Mark was born in Lufkin, Texas. Mark's mother was a single mother with three kids and all different fathers. He never met his father and his mother: never attended college, never had a stable job, and resorted to alcohol to provide her balance which led to a hopeless childhood. Mark's mother moved after his sophomore year in high school, so he was homeless and introduced to the street life hands-on at an early age. Although he found stability his senior year of high school to graduate, when Mr. Mark arrived at Prairie View he was another lost soul due to his lack of knowledge and information on higher learning.

Fortunately, Mr. Mark was able to get the right people in his life and make a glorifying transition. He is now passing his knowledge to other students around the world, to ensure that they are equipped with the tools to reach many levels of success. Mr. Mark is within the student's age range, so when he speaks, he's able to connect with them in a stronger and effective way. Today, he is actively seeking to speak and share his story and experiences to make an instilling impact on the lives of people everywhere!